TAKE THE LIMITS OFF OF
GOD!

Diane Ehrlich

REFORM MINISTRY PUBLICATIONS

Take The Limits Off Of God!

© 2011 by Diane Ehrlich

Published by Reform Ministry Publications
Cleveland, Ohio
www.reformministry.com

ISBN: 1460919793
ISBN-13: 9781460919798

"Be exalted, O God, above the heavens,
and let your glory be over all the earth."

Psalm 108:5 NIV

TABLE OF CONTENTS

ACKNOWLEDGEMENTS

The theme for this book appeared from out of the blue! One night at prayer meeting one of our prayer group members casually mentioned a catchy slogan she once heard, "Take the limits off of God!" The topic caught our interest and soon we were doing a weekly Bible study, uncovering ways that we were possibly limiting God, thereby frustrating His will.

I began to assemble notes from the study and the material for this book took form. As I composed each topic, I keenly sensed God's good pleasure and was convinced that the Lord wanted us to experience Him in a fuller way.

I would like to thank the many loving prayer partners who also sensed God's will and prayed accordingly. Thank to the Intercessory Prayer Team at Sanctuary Baptist Church who intercede faithfully for their fellow saints and community. I also want to acknowledge my parents, Harold and Melba Ehrlich for their unending support of all my projects. God's grace along with Christian teamwork once again proves to be an invincible combination.

INTRODUCTION

JESUS CALMS THE STORM

"How will God intervene during Desert Storm?" A couple of Jehovah Witnesses greeted me at my door and began probing my spiritual life with this jarring question. They were referring to America's involvement at the time with the war in Iraq against Saddam Hussein in 1989.

"He already has," I answered calmly. Their exchange of glances told me that they had not practiced for that particular answer. Caught off-guard, they decided to ignore my response and repeat the question.

"God already has intervened," I insisted. "God intervened in human history with the appearance of His Son, Jesus Christ. Christ was God's solution for our sinful condition. So the issue is not how God will stop this war—but whether or not we will accept His solution for our most basic problem."

Clearly frustrated that I would not change my beliefs, the couple soon left. Their approach had been to ignore God's plan in Christ to implement their own and I could not do that. Sadly, their strategy represents a common notion among people. We prefer to make up our minds about what God should do while ignoring the awesome potential of the foundational work He has already done. Many of us want a God who, like a dependable plow horse possesses formidable power, yet is tame and content to obey our

...he reins. This mythical mindset re-
...e we make Him up to be rather than
He really is.

...1 about God is totally backwards.
..."Follow Me" clearly defines who
...wers, we grow in our understanding
...is word and as we experience His activity.
...our personal implementation of the lessons He teaches us
is our way of accepting His leadership and lordship.

God's plan to change our war-torn planet has always
been to first change the human heart. The heart is the
decision center for every individual. Often, it is the place
where people wage personal war against God, against themselves and against others. **"For if, when we were God's enemies, we were reconciled to him through the death of his
Son..."** (Romans 5:10 NIV)

A change of heart is possible by the power of the indwelling Holy Spirit in the believer. By the Spirit, the Word of
God is brought to remembrance as situations arise, giving
God's people a new code to live by. The yielded Christlike
person can then be used to change a portion of his or her
world as God would desire. As Christian influence grows,
society can be significantly impacted by people who are
God's instruments of change. This is God's ideal plan in
Christ to calm the storm of man's inner and outer wars.

God has already intervened through Christ to address
man's plight and make Himself available to us with all
power. **"Therefore, since we have a great high priest who
has gone through the heavens, Jesus the Son of God, let
us hold firmly to the faith we profess. For we do not have
a high priest who is unable to sympathize with our weaknesses, but we have one who has been tempted in every
way, just as we are—yet was without sin."** (Hebrews 4: 14-15

NIV) As benefactors of a union with Christ, the possibilities for us are limitless!

Unfortunately, the enjoyment of God's presence and boundless power is not always our experience. In fact, there is a growing awareness in the Church of our need to tap into all that God has for us. Evidenced by the growing prayer movement, there is a restlessness that is prodding us to seek God for something more. Christians are aching for something undeniably real from the Spirit.

Recently I met with a women's ministry leader to discuss the theme for a weekend retreat. She commented that pressing circumstances in families seemed to be rallying church members to prayer.

"Wouldn't it be wonderful if our meetings were shaken by the invading presence of the Holy Spirit just like in the Book of Acts?" The scriptures verified God's willingness to visit with signs and wonders. We both knew the life-saving good that would result from God's visitation and held a short breath as we considered the possibilities of a meeting like that.

This train of thought provokes the question, "So what is holding God back?" If God has shown us accounts of His will to act with power, then why aren't we experiencing more of Heaven's refreshing? What unseen obstacles impede an outpouring of His Spirit on our behalf? Maybe the following story will give us a clue.

AN INSIDE JOB

"I believe it's an inside job!" The police detective drew his conclusion as he toured the church with the pastor after responding to a call about a robbery. The church secretary had come in that morning and discovered all the computer equipment gone. When the police arrived they noted that other valuables were missing such as sound equipment, microphones, a keyboard, a television and a VCR.

Strangely, there were no signs of breaking and entering. It became obvious that someone had cased the church looking for sellable items. That person must have hidden himself in the church after choir practice the night before. After choir members were gone, the thief methodically carried the items out the back door and drove away. The only explanation was that the thief had been a church member because it was clearly and inside job!

On a greater scale, I believe this incident speaks of another robbery going on within the Body of Christ. The Church seems to be robbed of its power and valuable spiritual impact, scrambling to prayer to find out why. By saying this, I'm not trying to discredit the work of God's servants who have given themselves to the ministry of the Gospel. I'm just doing some spiritual detective work as I compare what I see in scripture to what I see in churches I visit. If there is a dynamic supernatural grace of God's presence that seems to be missing, then I have to point to the human element and say, "I believe it's an inside job!"

TAKE THE LIMITS OFF OF GOD!

God has ordained human agency to carry out His purposes on earth. We are part of a "dynamic duo" as we co-labor with Christ. We know that God Himself is limitless, so we must be the limiting factor of the pair.

If we truly want more of what God has for us, then we need to discover for ourselves how we are being robbed of the spiritual impact that Christ has promised. The purpose of this book is to explore the possibilities of the riches that the Bible says are ours. If all God's promises are "Yes" in Christ, then what is necessary for the wonderful fulfillment of those promises? In what ways do we bind, halt or quench the work of the Holy Spirit who is our appointed heavenly Helper? How are we stopping God from making the necessary heart changes that He longs to make in order to use us to help change the world?

Through this book, I'll ask you to do your own detective work to obtain answers for those dire questions. As you read, you will come across challenging foundational truths followed by personal application questions. Take the time to ask God for His opinion before you answer them.

It is my burning desire that, as a benefactor of Christ, you will not be robbed of His blessing for any preventable reason. As a partner with Christ, I hope you will never hold Him back from gaining full access to your life. I pray that you will have the power to exert Christian influence wherever you go. And I hope that your insatiable hunger for God's supernatural manifest presence will compel you to make it your personal goal to ...TAKE THE LIMITS OFF OF GOD!

FAITHFULNESS

READ MATTHEW 25: 14-30

The three parables in Matthew 25 tell us that God highly values the gifts and resources He has entrusted to us. Our spiritual life in Christ is the most important aspect of our living and we would do well to devote our full attention to it. Jesus expects us not only to be active in our faith but also to be spiritually productive by showing a return for His investment at the Cross.

Faithfulness is an important trait because it indicates that a person's will has changed to serve God. Our actions will speak of a dedication to His eternal cause. Proven, faithful servants are of great value to God because they have passed a degree of testing and can be given important kingdom responsibilities that they will carry out.

Dependable servants will do the task that the Spirit prompts them to do. Commitments such as leading a Bible study, rehearsing for a musical performance or even setting up for a meeting will require the servant to come prepared, prayed-up and on time. The flow of responsibilities is much smoother when people do the job they have offered to do.

God's work is hindered by those who quit easily, back out of commitments or let people down by not showing up. Dependability is often more important than giftedness. People appreciate being able to rely on someone who is true to his word more that someone who is eloquent yet irresponsible.

Faithful people belong in a special category. Because they have proven themselves, they gain a reputation for their consistency to carry out what they say they will do. In relationships, faithful people remain loyal to others despite changing circumstances. A faithful friend or relative is always there for others no matter what. That kind of friendship is a great comfort to people because it offers a glimmer of stability in an unstable world. Faithful friends are often cherished more than words can express, thus setting them apart in the hearts of those they have helped.

The Bible says that the Lord has set the faithful apart for Himself. **"But know that the Lord has set apart the faithful for himself; the Lord hears when I call him."** (Psalm **4:3 NRSV**) I believe this is much like Honor Roll students who comprise a special segment of their high school class. Although they are with the rest of the class, they are set apart by the recognition of their superior dedication. In the same way, the faithful have God's attention because of the eagerness they have shown.

One of the names of Jesus is **"Faithful and True" (Revelation 9:11)** Followers who develop this trait are pleasing to Him. They become a human expression of God's own faithfulness and dependability, and therefore a credit to His character. This is one of the fruits of the Spirit that God desires in us. **(Galatians 5:22)**

It is God's will for us to leave our selfish, unreliable ways to become responsible adults who are able to take care of ourselves and others. Betrayal in families and among friends occurs when people bail out of relationships to better serve themselves. Jesus himself experienced the pain of betrayal and predicted that selfish motives would incite people to quit on each other. **"The love of most will grow**

cold." **(Matthew 24:12 NIV)** Unfaithfulness has a devastating effect on others, breaking bonds of trust and shattering sweet memories.

If we heed this warning, we can choose to be different from most people and keep love alive through faithfulness. We are promised that God will respond to our faith by showing Himself faithful. **(Psalm 18:25)** And our reward will be realized when we are personally congratulated by Christ for our demonstration of loyalty to Him through sheer belief in Him.

TAKE THE LIMITS OFF OF GOD
BY SHOWING YOURSELF FAITHFUL!

---

* How has Christ shown you that He wants you to serve Him?
* How have you responded?
* Do you faithfully fulfill your obligations to others?
* Are you in the habit of quitting easily?
* What ways can you become more faithful to Christ and to others?

ALLOWING GOD TO CHANGE US

READ GENESIS 32, 33:1-11

So often we cry out to God in prayer, asking Him to please change our relatives and friends. We should certainly pray for them, but more importantly we should also be asking God to change us. God is tremendously glorified when people adapt to Christ. His ability to change someone into a noticeably different person is undeniable evidence that He exists and has significant power. As we allow God to change us, then in an unexplainable way, Christ is released to work in the lives of friends and family members as well.

This principle of change is seen in the lives of Jacob and Esau. Jacob used deceit against his brother to gain his father's blessing. As a result, Esau plotted to kill his brother for stealing his blessing, and Jacob had to flee from home. For fourteen years Jacob labored for his uncle Laban. God prospered him with wives, children and livestock which was the upstart of the nation of Israel. But before this prophetic nation could be released to greatness, Jacob had to first go home to face his brother.

Still fearing for his life, Jacob turned to God in prayer, asking him to save him from his brother's anger. God responded to the plea to change Esau's heart by dealing with

Jacob's heart first. **"So Jacob was left alone, and a man wrestled with him till daybreak." (Genesis 32: 24 NIV)**

This wrestling match represents a season of change that God initiates to make us spiritual people. He has great plans for us, but we must be changed from our selfish, worldly, unspiritual ways that hinder Him. The Holy Spirit comes in close, convicting us of sin and using discipline to do a work of holiness. During this season of change, God may seem to be more like our worst enemy, but we must love Him for His discipline knowing that He will surely bless the spiritual life that He is bringing forth. God can only bless the Christ life within us when our minds are set on the things of the Spirit. As seen in Jacob, self nature is competitive, deceitful and a hindrance to God's purposes. In contrast, the spiritual life brings God's desires for ourselves and for others. Jacob's self-reliance had to be challenged and exchanged for a reliance on God's mercy. The wrestling match left Jacob exhausted and physically crippled, but he won his blessing from God! Now a different man, Israel headed out with the assurance that God would solve his differences with his brother.

Jacob looked up and saw Esau coming with his four hundred men. Had murder deepened in Esau so much that he would come against him with such an army? No—because God had time to work in his heart also. The once rash, ravenous Esau who allowed his appetite and emotions to rule him was now content with the portion of blessing that he had. **"But Esau said, 'I already have plenty, my brother. Keep what you have for yourself.'" (vs 9)** By the power of God, Esau was a changed man, too! Esau saw Jacob and ran to embrace him as the brothers wept in reconciliation.

Jesus told us that He expected change from those who come into His kingdom. **"And he said: 'I tell you the truth, unless you change and become like little children, you will**

never enter the kingdom of heaven." (Matthew 18:3 NIV)
God will take us in as we are, but He does not plan to leave
us that way!

The reason we allow God to change us is because we
want to please Him. **"So we make it our goal to please
him, whether we are at home in the body or away from it."
(2 Corinthians 5:10 NIV)** Out of love for Christ, we find out
what He likes and we change accordingly. **(Ephesians 5:10)**
We no longer live our life to please ourselves, but we want
to please God instead.

Christians halt God's changes when they choose to continue pleasing themselves. They may begin to do some basics like church-going and prayer in an attempt to make
some changes in their lives. But after a certain point, they
may stop and go no further, deciding that no further change
is necessary.

But for the Christian, change is growth. Spiritual growth
is not just about learning. It is how we apply our learning
to our living so that we live differently! We must see that
God had to change Jacob into Israel. He didn't just re-name
the same person. God had in mind to produce a nation
from that person. God is able to change selfish sinners into
selfless, serving saints, revealing the new creatures that we
actually are in Christ. We must be open and willing to accept the changes that God wants to bring so that we will be
noticeably different people to our family and friends.

TAKE THE LIMITS OFF OF GOD BY ALLOWING GOD TO
CHANGE US!

---

* How often do you pray for family members?
* Are you first willing to see how you need to change?

* Have you sincerely asked God to make the changes He wants for your life?
* Will you stop trying to change others and allow God to deal with you instead?

GODLY LOV

READ 1 CORINTHIANS 13: 1-13

The "love chapter" in 1 Corinthians 13 is often read at wedding ceremonies as an ideal for the newly wed couple to live by. It is a poetic reminder of how enjoyable human relationships can be when we try to be considerate of others. From this chapter, we can easily see that there is no higher way to live than to love.

But the practice of godly love on a daily basis as we encounter our fellow man is an immense challenge. This is difficult for us mainly because we are not loving by nature. In fact, we must restrain our true mean, ugly nature and draw upon the power of Christ to help us to love. Godly love, then, is not a flowery ideal disassociated with reality, but a daily moral choice of how we are going to treat others. It is a practical path to choose rather than temporary feelings to feel. As we play our part in each relational exchange, godly love is more about giving than getting, putting others first before ourselves.

In contrast, humanistic love is based on lust, which is a craving for something for ourselves. We say we love someone because we see how that person can help fulfill our perceived need. In this way, we love someone for what he or she can do for us as an extension of our own self-love.

Godly love is a more mature, responsible love that has no motive except for what matters for someone else.

15

became a man, I put childish ways behind me."
rinthians 13:11 NIV) When we become accomplished
love, we expect nothing in return nor do we demand re-
payment. We agree to follow Christ as He walks us through
the depths and dangers of loving others who don't neces-
sarily love us back, bravely extending ourselves as human
vessels of God's love.

To get the most out of the "love chapter," let's para-
phrase the verses in such a way that we truly understand
the appeal that scripture is making. Then we can approach
people with a readiness in our hearts to respond to them
with godly love.

"When we choose to love, we catch ourselves being
mean to other people and we stop it! We tell ourselves
that meanness is not a loving way. We remind ourselves that
other people are going through difficulties that we are not
aware of, so we should not compound their problems with
a rough, harsh manner."

"When we choose to love, we refuse the temptation of
hating others for what they seem to have. Self-centered
comparing and angry jealousy don't do anyone any good.
Instead, when we see others doing well, we should be glad
for them. We should want God's goodness to be felt in everyone's life. Then when we get a breakthrough, we should
not go around bragging, but express our happiness through
a grateful, humble attitude."

"When we choose to love, we work to rid ourselves of
stubbornness that insists on having its own way all of the
time. We learn the give and take of relationships by letting
go and honoring other people's wishes."

"When we choose to love, we do not lash out at others to
express our change in mood swings. Venting our feelings is
not what others are for. And we do not keep offenses alive

in our mind, ready to bring them up later. This self-defense tactic is harmful to those we say we love."

"When we choose to love, we do not take pleasure in sins of the tongue such as gossip, malicious talk or haughty opinions. Instead, we want God's truth to come to the forefront in our thinking and speech, and we will deal with others honestly and openly."

"When we choose to love, we try to bear up under difficult personalities and believe that people can change. We always hope for the best for people while using wisdom. We pray that people will come through with victory during tough times, and we will show our loyalty to them unless God shows us to let the relationship go."

"Faith, hope and love for others builds people up and brings lasting results. If we can remember always to choose the loving way, we can have greatness of character. And surely God can use us to reach out to others because we are walking in Christ's footsteps when we choose to love."

TAKE THE LIMITS OFF OF GOD THROUGH GODLY LOVE!

---

* What things do you catch yourself doing that are not loving?
* What are you like towards people when you don't get your own way?
* How do you prefer to be treated? Do you treat others the same way?
* Who do you need to show more love to?

TRUE FASTING

READ ISAIAH 58: 1-11

In this passage, God gives a clear explanation why He is withholding His blessing. He tells Israel that their fasting is a farce! Outwardly, they seem to be seeking God. **"For day after day they seek me out; they seem eager to know my ways." (vs 2)** But their arguing and striking out against each other behind closed doors betrays their humble public plea. As a result, God shuts off Heaven's help and insists on an attitude improvement before He will move.

This is a sobering spiritual principle that we need to take an honest look at. We should never insult the intelligence of God by thinking that He doesn't know the true motives behind our behavior. The truth is that we live before God's eyes every moment. Just because we can't see Him doesn't mean that He can't see us! As an observant Father, He intently watches everything we do and listens to everything we say. Looking over our shoulder to see who is nearby and lowering our voices to a whisper doesn't conceal our actions from Him.

God would not respond to Israel's fast because they were using human force to get what they wanted rather than waiting for God to move on their behalf. Human force is the power people use to exert their human spirit in an aggressive way to make others do what they want. In his fallen state, man acquired a working knowledge of evil enabling him to think up wrongly motivated schemes to achieve his own goals. The sin element supplies the power to produce human force. Passive aggression is when we vent our anger and ill-will at someone in a polite way. We level soulish power at someone to bring pain but we just clean it up so that it won't seem too bad!

Here are some common uses of human force that you may be familiar with:

- Guilt Trips
- Mind Games
- Demanding/controlling ways
- Mean, sarcastic language
- Yelling
- Accusation
- Nagging
- Judgmental attitudes

All these ways are selfish and unloving, dishonoring God when we use them.

A spirit of man prevails in a home or even in a church when people shun the power and presence of the Holy Spirit, opting for soulish power instead. The spirit of man is a very oppressive spirit that fosters tyranny and occurs when people trust in their own schemes rather than innocently trusting God. Because God's Spirit is so unwelcome, the atmosphere is very dry and unloving. People bicker at meetings and ministry is difficult, yet people maintain a haughty pride about what they are doing.

God is aware of how we oppress one another emotionally and then point the finger of blame at others. **(vs 9)** The "pointing finger" suggests how easily we pay attention to other people's sins, yet neglect to see our own. When we point out other people's wrong doings with disdainful criticism then we become huffy and self-righteous. God says that we hold back His visitation because we assume His place as God and Judge of all. We bring judgment on ourselves when we judge the sins of others yet do the same thing. **(Romans 2:2-3)** Our prideful pointing plays right into the devil's plan as we become part of the oppressive atmosphere.

How can we expect God to move in our churches on Sunday morning as we lift our hands in worship, yet throughout the week we lift our voices in anger, bitterness and blame to others? Christians need to take their religion home with them and stop trashing it in the lobby along with the church bulletin on the way out the door! We don't fool God! His Spirit is not confined to the church building as we might hope! The Spirit is grieved when people rely on aggressive human force rather than trusting God to come forth with the daily power that they need. For God to respond to our fasting, we need to stop our obsession with other people's lives and start living up to our own moral responsibility!

The discipline of fasting is meant to be an outward sign to God of inward repentance. Fasting declares physically that we feel so bad about sin that we have lost our appetite. When we disagree with sin and Satan that much, then God will see our true motives and will come with delivering power to break the grip of evil. **"Submit yourselves, then, to God. Resist the devil, and he will flee from you." (James 4:7 NIV)** Combined with prayer, fasting is a very effective weapon of spiritual warfare. Our active protest of sin unites us with the Holy Spirit in His cause to evict the powers of darkness that influence and oppress people.

Fasting is also a sign to God that we are seeking His will and direction. It is a spiritual act that dispels confusion and achieves clarity. Fasting is a form of asking. The silent physical hunger that we purposely feel tells God that we hunger for His answers.

God loves to give spiritual breakthroughs! His answers scatter darkness like daybreak. **(vs 8)** God is willing to give radiant power to remove our spiritual oppressors. He says that He gladly makes our spiritual life like a bright, sunny day! **(vs 10)** When we clean up our attitudes towards each other, then we can welcome God's presence through true fasting.

Our loving Heavenly Father wants to protect us and refresh us with His glorious power, not wishing to withhold from us any of His blessing!

TAKE THE LIMITS OFF OF GOD
THROUGH TRUE FASTING!

---

* In what ways are you using human force and passive aggression against others to solve your problems?
* Will you trust God for His daily power to help you?
* What area of your life do you need a spiritual breakthrough?
* Try skipping a meal and use that time to pray. Don't tell anyone what you are doing. Keep seeking God until you sense His presence.

THE DELUSION OF SELF

READ 2 THESSALONIANS 2:1-11

Do you ever wonder what drives people to do some of the sick-minded things that they do? I believe that most of the trouble in our world comes from people thoughtlessly and ruthlessly serving themselves. A prime example was the Romanian dictator Nicolae Ceusesu who emerged from the Communist ranks and successfully dashed the hopes and ruined the lives of the country's working class, forcing them to serve his own selfish aspirations. "Ceausescu climbed through the party ranks, dreaming of the day Romania would be his. By the early 1970's his dream had come true. He was president of Romania, with the party and the army firmly behind him...Ruling from a kitschy Versailles-style palace in Bucharest, he brutally plundered Romania and reshaped it in his own sick image."[1] What would cause a person to starve a whole country just to feed his own ego? Unfortunately, the potential to do the very same thing resides deep within every human being.

With spiritual eyes, John the Baptist saw into the depths of human selfishness while under the power of the Holy Spirit. First he saw the self-centered evil that grips the hearts of people. Then he saw Jesus as God. **"I have seen and I testify this is the Son of God." (John 1: 34 NIV)** Just as John prepared the way for Christ's initial visit, the preparation

---

1   *The Body,* P. 40

23

Christ's return will require the Church to
he same two things.
e truly see self as an evil that we need to
can we lift our eyes and see the true God
and replace us. We must ask ourselves who
we are really trusting in—ourselves or Jesus? Where does
our real hope lie and who supplies our daily strength? Our
answers to these questions determine how we cope with
each day, especially when we face difficulties.

If our trust is not absolutely in Jesus, then we run the risk
of being so filled with self-glory that our self love blocks our
view of Christ. This Bible text mentions **"a powerful delusion so that they will believe the lie..." (vs 11)** This refers
to the original lie that Adam believed, rejecting the truth
and seeking a way to bypass the rule of God to become his
own "god." Adam denied his need of God's guidance and
sought to live his life independently. This is the delusion of
self.

Throwing off God's rule does not give us real freedom.
Instead, we are caught up in our own foolish whims, and
like a tiny prison cell, self-life becomes our world. We are
locked into wrong ways that originate in our own minds and
make poor, misguided choices at every turn. But as long as
we are proud of how we are running our own life, we will
not accept the excellence of God's rule. Then we will limp
through life with no healing, refusing to see Jesus as One
who is greater than ourselves.

This stubborn mindset is at work deluding people
today. **"For the secret power of lawlessness is already at
work." (vs 7)** People may admit that God exists, but they
deny their need of His guidance and personal rule. The
original lie has taken hold in people's belief system and
takes the form of "personal truth" or "what is true for me."
Youth culture specialist Josh McDowell speaks from his

research on the beliefs of young people, "Today, truth is not there to be discovered. Truth is there to be 'created'... Today all truth is personal opinion."[2] His findings tell us that the void of understanding God's truth in our culture has extended an invitation for people to make up their own "truth."

Although their beliefs originate from self-life, they value, live by and defend their system of truths and, like the Romanian dictator, justify everything they decide to do. This is the reasoning that **"finds delight in wickedness" (vs 2)** that God warns us to avoid.

A delusion is defined as a misconception, a false impression, a dream world, a fantasy and a hoax. Christians must refuse to live in a delusion of self. Like John the Baptist, we must see self-life as a barrier to God and therefore an enemy of our faith. Focusing on self is a distraction from seeing Jesus.

As we see Him, we will become like Him. Christ is the One to be revealed in us. He is the One who is to be seen, heard and marveled at, not us! We need to see Jesus as God ruling over everything we think, say and do. We need to see Him as God over all circumstances, over all people and over all the earth.

The prophet Daniel clearly saw God in a vision. **"As I watched, thrones were set in place, and an Ancient One took his throne..." (Daniel 7:9 NRSV)** Daniel then saw the beast who was speaking arrogantly against God put to death and his body destroyed. Just as Jesus has a "body" on earth, so does Anti-Christ have a "body" on earth. His "body" is made up of people who speak arrogantly in their minds and hearts against God and follow the powerful delusion of self. Their end is destruction.

---

2   *Josh McDowell*, 1999

Surrounding God's throne are **"a thousand thousands" (Daniel 7:10 NRSV)** who worship and serve Him. Not only do we need to see Jesus as God, we need to love Him, worship Him and be one of the many thousands who serve Him with all of our hearts. **"I am the Lord your God, who brought you out of Egypt, out of the land of slavery. You shall have no other gods before me." (Exodus 20: 1-2 NIV)** When we deny the evil intentions of self-life, we can rejoice in serving a great and mighty God with no regrets.

TAKE THE LIMITS OFF OF GOD BY
UNDERSTANDING THE DELUSION OF SELF!

---

* What do you see yourself demanding of others? Time, attention, their service to you?
* What areas of your life have you resisted the rule of Christ?
* Do you have a holy fear of Jesus as God and a healthy refusal of the ways of self?
* How are you serving Christ as an act of worship of Him?

BE A BLESSING—NOT A BURDEN

READ GENESIS 12: 1-7

God's way has always been to win people's hearts by overwhelming them with His personal love for them. God originally intended to win the affections of the people on earth through the nation of Israel. The pagan nations would see for themselves how good, powerful and superior Israel's God was, and they would want Him instead of their gods. This nation was meant to be so obviously rich in the blessings of God that they would become a source of relief and freedom rather than a burdensome oppressor. **"For the Lord your God is God of gods and Lord of lords, the great God, mighty and awesome, who shows no partiality and accepts no bribes. He defends the cause of the father-less and widow, and loves the alien, giving him food and clothing. And you are to love those who are aliens, for you yourselves were aliens in Egypt." (Deuteronomy 10: 18-19 NIV)** Ideally, out of love and service to God, Israel would sacrificially use their blessing to bless others.

This is no less the vision God has for the nation of believ-ers in Christ today. As Israel once followed the Cloud of Glory, so we now follow the leading of the Holy Spirit. Fully God Himself, the Spirit continuously works to bring us into activities that are meant to bless others. He wants to help us develop a selfless lifestyle. Because God is always working to make Himself known through His goodness, the influence of the Church should be felt by the world.

For example, I was in the store one Saturday and watched an active two year old reach for something while seated in the grocery cart. Climbing up on his knees now, he was about to take a fall when I spoke a word to his mother who stopped him just in time. There was no real obligation for me to get involved. He was not my child, and I could have turned my back and hoped for the best. But I am obligated to God through a love covenant. I know that I am to do what is right, to bring aid and comfort to others because that best expresses the Father's heart. So I extend myself, going out of my way, to bring God's kindness to people.

Unfortunately many believers have refused God's vision of unselfish responsibility towards others. In fact, many people are a burden rather than God's intended blessing. A burden is a weight, a hindrance, a worry, a grief, or a load that is heavy to carry. Not speaking of physical disabilities, many Christians fit into this category. Some purposely neglect their responsibilities, causing an additional load for someone else. Others are just plain lazy, refusing to work for a living or perhaps remain underemployed because that is an easy, safe way to live.

Others struggle with sin issues for years, never admitting to themselves that they have a problem yet they are constantly suffering because of their own wrong attitudes. The problems of those living in disobedience will automatically spill over and adversely affect people around them. Sometimes Christians are emotionally immature and become somewhat flaky in their spirituality. They lose their effectiveness because they have not become mature enough to live in the world yet not of it.

If Christians would sober up about God's intentions to use us, surely we could be raised up to a place of stability in character and circumstances to be able to bless others. The meaning of bless is to give something to, to bring joy, to encourage, to build up and to add good fortune to. If we do anything as Christians, we should help lighten the load of others, not add to it! We become a blessing when our mind starts to operate with that intention, looking for ways to help others. We don't have to look far because opportunities are all around us.

We can bless others through godly words combined with sensitive timing. **"The Sovereign Lord has given me an instructed tongue, to know the word that sustains the weary." (Isaiah 50: 4 NIV)** We can also choose to forgive and to bless in response to offenses. **(1 Peter 3:9)** Or we may serve in ways to show simple kindness and thoughtfulness. Otherwise, we may share material resources, financial aid, food, clothing or household goods.

Actively blessing others sets the spiritual tone of a relationship, paving the way for people to come to know Christ. In our natural world, most people are always grabbing for themselves. In contrast, sacrificial living becomes an attention-getter. **"God's kindness leads you towards repentance." (Romans 2:4 NIV)** Christians who see the importance of reaching out to others and who incorporate that into their daily living prove that they understand God's ultimate will to reveal Jesus Christ as Savior of the world. Christians will be given great and unusual blessings only as they position themselves as God's eager stewards with the intention of blessing others as they are blessed.

TAKE THE LIMITS OFF OF GOD BY BEING
A BLESSING—NOT A BURDEN!

---

* How do you view your material possessions—as God's or your own to keep?
* Have you been a burden for anyone in your circle of family, friends, co-workers?
* Is giving a joy or grief to you?
* How can you make your Christian faith be felt by others through blessing?

WE NEED GOD'S TEACHING AND HIS TOUCHING

READ JOHN 14: 15-27

In this passage, Jesus prepares His disciples to receive the Holy Spirit. He gives them a teaching to reassure them of His relationship with God the Father and explains that the Spirit would come from the Father in Jesus' name. Jesus carefully prepared them with teaching so that, when the experience occurred, they would not refuse the Spirit's "touching." This shows us that God wants us to have His teaching and His touching. We must see that education about God and experience with God are both from Him.

The Holy Spirit was sent as the Divine Escort to bring the Church through this present evil age. The Son completed His duty to the Father in dying for the sins of mankind and establishing a new race upon the earth. The Spirit's duty to the Father is to promote the saving work of the Son, to re-create man through the spiritual birth, to protect the Church from the devil, to train God's people in His ways, to empower them to do His will, and to prepare them in holiness to someday unite with the Son. The Holy Spirit is now the Person of God that we interact with in our spiritual life.

Our Counselor teaches and reminds us of the words of Jesus. Personal Bible reading and group Bible study are perfect ways to learn the Word of God, giving the Holy Spirit more truth to bring to mind when we need it. We need to be taught sound doctrine to get the right meaning from the Bible's spiritual language. But the Spirit's goal is not just to educate us. His goal is to transform us!

One of the most detrimental results of the Fall was man's habit of covering up wrong doing rather than admitting the truth. The deep stain of pride induces people to be secretive, hiding their sin in self-defense behind lies of selfish reasoning. People avoid the presence of God in order to keep their secrets buried and untouched. **"I heard you in the garden and I was afraid...so I hid." (Genesis 3:10 NIV)**

The heart of man is truly a touchy subject. Much pain, unresolved hard feelings and fear reside within our hearts. Often we would rather hold on to these things and remain in control rather than face an unexpected catalyst that might trigger exposure.

In order to minister effectively, the Spirit of God works to open people's hearts from being closed to God because of secret, sinful hiding. **"But whoever lives by the truth comes into the light, so it may be seen plainly what he has done..." (John 3:21 NIV)** The Word of God is called the Sword of the Spirit because the Spirit uses it to strike the heart open and expose the lies buried inside of us. Then we can come out from behind our hiding places and gain a sense of real release and resolve. **"For the prince of this world is coming. He has no hold on me." (John 14: 3 NIV)**

The Spirit is the only one powerful yet gentle enough to deal with man's heart. He knows how much truth we can bear and is careful not to do harmful damage. But we need to love the truth and welcome His presence in order for this to happen.

There is nothing wrong with wanting an experiential touch from God. We should open ourselves us to the full ministry of the Holy Spirit, letting Him accomplish in us all He was sent to do. To be overly rigid and avoid any atmosphere where the Spirit is felt is like saying to God, "You can teach me...but you can't touch me!" Protecting ourselves from the healing touch that God wants to bring only reinforces inner hideouts with stubborn resistance.

When the Spirit is given the freedom to move in our midst, then people increase in their faith by their experience of the reality of God. **"...He will be convinced by all that he is a sinner and will be judged by all, and the secrets of his heart will be laid bare. So he will fall down and worship God, exclaiming, 'God is really among you!'"** **(1 Corinthians 14:25 NIV)** The Spirit of God comes in to our midst not only to teach but also to touch our hearts with conviction. **"Our gospel came to you not simply with words, but also with power, with the Holy Spirit and with deep conviction." (1 Thessalonians 1:4-5 NIV)** The presence of God through the Spirit works to enlighten our hearts and draw us into a closer relationship with the Father. This is the life-changing work that the Spirit is duty-bound to the Father to do.

We need to release ourselves to the ministry of the Spirit, purposely telling God that we want to open our hearts to Him. Stop holding back to protect yourself and ask Him to show you your own secrets. Give God permission to do as He wishes and invite Him to teach you and to touch you. See how good it is to open yourself to the presence of God and not avoid Him, so that you can experience a measure of His reality. When we do this, we can quit our shameful hiding and step out to become the expression of Christ that the Spirit wants to make us to be!

TAKE THE LIMITS OFF OF GOD THROUGH GOD'S TEACHING AND HIS TOUCHING!

---

* Tell God your deepest secrets. He already knows them!
* Do you approach God with childlike openness or reserved control?
* What specific area in your life needs a healing touch from God?
* Will you ask Him to touch you in such a way that you will know that you have been touched?

OUR PRIVILEGE OF PRAYER

READ ISAIAH 56: 1-8

If a famous billionaire walked up to you and said "Ask me for anything and I will give you your request!" you would most likely jump at the chance to tell him your request, knowing that he could make his promise good! Why is it, then, when the God of the universe says to us "Just ask me and I will give it to you!" we lack the same excitement to take advantage of His offer?

Admittedly, God has added a disclaimer clause to that offer. Tacked on to "whatsoever" is a qualifying phrase that says **"according to His will"** (1 **John 5:14**) But is that any reason to be disheartened? Even with that qualifier, we should still be enthusiastic about what God will do through prayer. He does not want to discourage our asking. Even with that qualifier, we should be enthusiastic about what God will do through prayer. By accepting that condition, we should still believe that our prayers are limitless.

God is merely protecting us by filtering His power that is accessed in prayer through His will. If we had unlimited say-so with divine power, our unenlightened hearts would ask amiss, and do great damage to ourselves and others. Even so, we should not become disenchanted with the possibilities of prayer just because God has chosen to properly monitor His awesome power. God simply reserves the right to have the final say as to how and when prayer will be answered. **(James 5: 16-18)**

We must go on believing that our circumstances will improve as God touches through prayer. Answers to hard questions suddenly pop into our head and the direction we need to take becomes obvious. When we remember to pray, the day's activities line up, money and provisions find their way to us, and relationships go much smoother.

I believe many Christians have yet to understand the benefit of seeking the counsel of God through prayer. The privilege of prayer given to every Christian carries enormous potential for power, change and relief, yet often remains unused. I suspect that Christians resist prayer for three main reasons:

1) They simply don't believe that prayer does much good or they give up believing when answers don't come quickly.
2) Prayer is bidding the Holy Spirit to move. The flesh would rather remain in control rather than relinquish control to the Holy Spirit. People resist prayer because they resist having to comply with the Holy Spirit.
3) Unforgiveness causes people to have such hard feelings against others that they cannot pray for them.

To give ourselves to prayer, we must become totally convinced that God has a better way to work things out. We must humble ourselves to ask God to do us a favor. As a result, prayer creates a supernatural atmosphere that invokes the presence of the Almighty on behalf of the lowly. Prayer is the incense burnt upon the altar of the hearts of the saints that ascends to the very throne room of God.

This is the spiritual conference call that makes Heaven so immediately near. And during that time of prayer, God's spirit realm joins and overwhelms our natural realm as the glory comes down!

In our study verse, God encourages us to pray by promising that He will give us **"joy in my house of prayer." (vs 7)** The sacrifice of prayer is gladly accepted by God. His will is for His people to beckon His presence so much through prayer that their places of worship will be known as **"a house of prayer." (vs 7)** As Christians, we need to stretch ourselves, first in believing and then in submitting as we take advantage of our wonderful privilege of prayer.

TAKE THE LIMITS OFF OF GOD THROUGH THE PRIVILEGE OF PRAYER!

---

* How often do you pray during the week? Confess the things that hinder you.
* Does prayer seem like a hard task or is it a joy?
* What answers do you know you have received through prayer?
* Will you give yourself to prayer in a new way?

PERSONAL HOLINESS

READ JOSHUA 6:27, 7:1-26

Sin absolutely robs Christians of their rightful spiritual power. Again and again I hear of Christians who are seeking guidance through astrology, psychics and fortune tellers. Participation in these entry-level occult practices are clearly forbidden by scripture. **"Let no one be found among you who sacrifices his son or daughter in the fire, who practices divination or sorcery, interprets omens, engages in witchcraft, or casts spells or who is a medium or spiritist or who consults the dead. Anyone who does these things is detestable to the Lord..." (Deuteronomy 18: 10-12 NIV)** Yet for some reason, people go along with these evil practices thinking that they are just for "fun!"

Attention Christians! Supernatural evil is not a game! The devil plays for high stakes, and he counts on people's foolish ignorance to keep the losses rolling in, life by ruined life. If Christians would accept the truth about how real and personal the devil is, and see that they are the only people who can effectively counter him then the spiritual climate in our country would turn around much more quickly! But as long as God's own people hold onto the devil's ways, their spiritual influence with Heaven is cut way short.

This passage teaches us the principle of "legal ground," which is the rightful permission granted to the enemy to use his power against us due to un-confessed, un-renounced sin.

In this reading, God was with Joshua as mightily as He was with Moses. God's will was to use Israel to take the Promised Land by force. By now, Israel had the training, experience and courage to do it. Joshua sent men to spy on the city of Ai, and the report came back that it was an easy win. Yet with all these advantages in place, Israel was sorely defeated and now had to fear repercussion from hostile nations all around them. What went wrong?

Achan, one of the Israelite men, had taken some of the forbidden treasures after the defeat of the city of Jericho and buried them under his tent. The offense of one man's disobedience against God effectively shut down the anointing that God had for the battle against Ai. Israel was robbed of the victory that was meant to be theirs. **"Israel has sinned... they have stolen, they have lied...that is why Israel cannot stand against their enemies." (vs 11-12)**

I learned the reality of the principle of "legal ground" early in my Christian walk. I had been witnessing to a young college student who had made friends with some Satan worshippers while on campus. He quit school and moved home many miles away from them. Even so, he was plagued with tormenting suicidal thoughts.

Because I was taking him to church with me, the demons he carried were attacking me with an oppressive chronic fatigue. I prayed and prayed, commanding the spirits to go but they wouldn't leave. I asked God why they wouldn't obey me. God gently impressed upon me that, as a new Christian fresh out of the world, I had too much "legal ground" of sin in me that was robbing me of the spiritual power that I needed. Eventually, the young man accepted Christ, and the evil forces left me because they had lost him. That experience launched me onto an eager path of personal holiness and today I have success in spiritual warfare that puts me on terms with Joshua!

This scripture keenly demonstrates why Christians often lead powerless, defeated lives. The buried possessions of Achan represent disobedience to God's Word. Unredeemed, un-surrendered, unenlightened areas in our heart give the enemy opportunities to use his power against us. Christians can be plagued by unusual chronic fatigue, depression, defeat, discouragement and a sense of futility because they are literally being held down from within.

The enemy works to convince us of the advantages of keeping the sin. He maintains legal permission as long as the Christian loves the sin above God's Word. If that sin is treasured in the person's heart so that he is devoted to it and wished to keep it, then he stand in side-by-side agreement with the devil in resistance to God's will. The devil can point to that beloved sin and say to God, "Ha! Ha! That Christian agrees with me—not you! I can stay because you do not force man's will!" God must withhold His power due to that claim. These are real spiritual dynamics that we must believe and know.

If we seek God to show us the truth about our own hearts, He will expose areas of sin and we will be cleansed. God will drive out the enemies He finds working against us as the Holy Spirit comes to take over the "Promised Land" of our lives. **"But if I drive demons by the finger of God, then the kingdom of God has come to you." (Luke 11: 20 NIV)** Many times people will feel a sudden lightness or sense of relief when they pray, as if something has been lifted off of them. This is evidence of God working to remove enemy strongholds.

Not only do we need to value our emotional well-being, we also need to value God's anointing. Holiness and personal purity are major keys to having spiritual power. After a season of concentrated personal repentance, a Christian should be able to say to some degree, **"For the prince of this world is coming. He has no hold on me..." (John 14: 30 NIV)**

The famous evangelist Charles Finney was a living example of this spiritual principle. It was said of his personal power that, when he opened his mouth to speak, "bombardment began!" Church history documents that "the effects of his speaking were almost unparalleled in modern history. Over half a million people were converted through his ministry."[3]

Ideally, all Christians should be super-charged with God's power. The Church is ordained by God to expand and take the "Promised Land" of human hearts for Jesus Christ. When Christians talk to unbelievers about issues of faith, people should come under a degree of conviction. Devils should be in an uproar constantly about us, yet they cannot touch us because of holiness and prayer. Most of all, Christians should be able to move into higher levels of Christian service without being plagued by pesky enemy forces.

Like Joshua, God is with us! We possess every advantage to promote Jesus Christ and help people to change their lives. We must be in faith for God's power, but we must also do our part to meet God's conditions of holiness to receive it.

TAKE THE LIMITS OFF OF GOD THROUGH PERSONAL HOLINESS!

---

*   Do you have any specific sins that you treasure above God's Word?

---

3   *Revival,* P. 136

* Are you experiencing any symptoms of chronic fatigue, depression or discouragement that may be spiritual in nature?
* Do you see the importance of having God's power operating in your life?
* Will you seek God to make a new commitment to personal holiness?

LIVING IN LIGHT OF FINAL JUDGMENT

READ ROMANS 2:5-11

A neighbor was walking her dog on a leash one day while I was outside. For some reason, the dog went into a frenzy when it saw me, barking viciously. It almost choked itself trying to get at me. The neighbor was embarrassed at the silliness of the dog. How could it have possibly thought it could attack me and win when it only weighed 15 lbs. or less? Somehow it considered itself to be bigger than me!

This incident speaks of man's inflated ego about himself. In the same way, people are dreadfully deceived in thinking that no one is "bigger" than them. Imagining ourselves to be invincible, we think that we are much greater, smarter and more powerful than we truly are.

The truth of final judgment brings man's puffed-up opinion of himself acutely into perspective. With a clear understanding of how God will review the final account of every life ever lived, our self-deception would be sharply halted. God has informed us of a final judgment so that we will radically change our view of this earthy life to inspire us to live in preparation for that incredible day. The present age would no longer captivate our attention. Instead, the promise of the future would be our incentive to make every day count for God.

God says that every living soul belongs to Him. God has rightful, legal ownership of every person as their Maker who gave them life. But God also gave man free moral choice with a warning that separation from Him would be the consequence of disobedience to Him. God then patiently waits as human history is played out, continuing to allow free moral choice to all who live in this world. He has destined a time when He will judge the lives of all people on the basis of their claim of Him as their God. **"Rise up, O God, judge the earth, for all the nations are your inheritance." (Psalm 82:8 NIV)**

When this age comes to a close and human existence in this world ends, the accounts of all lives will be opened and **"the dead were judged according to what they had done as recorded in the books." (Revelation 20: 12 NIV)** People who have not received Jesus Christ as Savior will be judged for their sins and they will fully know what they are being punished for. Those who received Jesus Christ as Savior have their names written in the Book of Life and they will not receive punishment, but a pardon instead.

That gracious pardon does not let us off the hook of accountability for how we choose to live our Christian life. Some day each believer will also face Jesus, as an instant replay of our life will be displayed. We will stand before the One who deserves the worship of all creation and our life will tell if we truly worshipped Him. On the basis of His demonstration of His love for us on Calvary, He will want to know how much we loved Him back through obedience to Him.

In the Bible there is plenty of clear teaching about the upcoming final judgment. It should not be a surprise ending for any Christian. This peek into the future should serve as sufficient warning for us to use our free moral choice as a means to expressing our gratitude to the One who died for us. Living in preparation for that momentous event should not only deter us from making serious sinful mistakes, but also encourage us to live for success in Heaven. We have time to love and serve Christ so we can look forward to His commendation of us.

As loyal believers, we can look beyond the standards of this natural world and be glad that the final judgment will be the ultimate victory for our God! The Judgment will be a final display for all created beings—human, angelic and demonic—that Jesus Christ is Lord of all! It will be the final proving ground, dispelling all self-deception, showing everyone that He has ultimate authority, undisputed power, and final dispensation of our eternal future. The assembly of souls will form a public arena that will end all rebellion against God as **"every mouth will be silenced and the whole world held accountable to God. (Romans 3:19 NIV)** And we will join Him as He delegates responsibility to us in proportion to the preparation we have made in ourselves on earth.

If we would take truth of this future to heart and live in a right fear of the Almighty Living God, then we should live the one life God has given us according to His wishes. The godly moral choices we make very single day will bring us great joy and satisfaction on that final day.

TAKE THE LIMITS OFF OF GOD BY LIVING IN LIGHT OF
FINAL JUDGMENT!

---

* God has a perfect will or plan in mind for your life. Are you on His plan?

* Do you have a comfortable, nonchalant, flip attitude towards God, or do you have a healthy, reverent fear?
* What changes do you need to make to be ready for Judgment Day?
* If you have nothing else to be glad about in your life right now—be glad that your name is written in the Lamb's Book of Life.

GODLY SORROW

READ EZEKIEL 9:1-11

Early one Sunday morning I drove to a nearby shopping center to withdraw some cash from the bank machine. A handful of early shoppers whisked in and out among scattered grocery carts. I looked across the lot and saw a wild looking blonde nervously glancing back and forth, looking to see if anyone was watching her. The open pavement offered no camouflage as she stood yanking out handfuls of golden day lilies that were blooming in the parking lot island. I pulled my station wagon slowly alongside to confront her as she was about to escape with her stolen bouquet.

"God sees what you are doing!" I spoke from the car window. I caught her bloodshot eyes with my solemn stare. Then I repeated myself to give conviction a chance to set in.

"Hey, my old man just died!" she shouted back. Her girlfriends stifled their giggles, deliriously proud of their hero's quick thinking.

"I'm sorry," I said as I drove away. I had no snappy comeback like she did.

Why, though, did I tell her I was sorry? I knew she was lying because she got caught. But a part of me was sorry for what I just seen. I was sorry that, bright and early Sunday morning, God's day was being dishonored and those young women were out wasting their lives on whatever reckless damage they could get away with. I read newspaper headlines about people wasting their lives on crime and taking others down with them and I become sadder and sorrier.

Along with her loss of conscience, America at this moment in history seems to have missed her calling. So much emphasis has been placed on entertainment in our culture that planet earth seems to have become our playground more than our mission field. Soul searching and rugged self-examination are passé. We have no time for it. We must keep the entertainment going.

In the Old Testament, the city of Jerusalem had also missed her calling. The Spirit of God showed the prophet Ezekiel in a vision the abominable worship that was going on in the temple behind closed doors. God could no longer tolerate the idolatry in Jerusalem because the conscience of church leadership was silent. They said to themselves, **"The Lord does not see." (Ezekiel 9:9 NIV)** They were aware of the existence of God, but they didn't care what His standards were for the nation.

As the angel went out into the city, he found a group of people who were in touch with the heart of God and did care about His standards. These people were privately grieved at the offensive worship and lamented the nation's sin against God. **(Ezekiel 9:4)** They were marked with a seal because of their godly sorrow.

If the Church in America carries any vision to rebuild the protective walls of moral decency that have been torn down by men and women who have publicly flaunted their sin, then a private assembly must gather before God to express their dissatisfaction and gut-level godly sorrow. Conviction power released by the Spirit of God is our only hope of penetrating America's hardened conscience.

Two seemingly opposite principles can be combined for effective intercession for our country: boldness and humility. The first is seen in the parable of the persistent widow. **(Luke 18:1-8)** This determined little lady kept coming to the judge with her plea, **"Grant me justice against my adversary."** **(vs 33)** Justice is the use of authority to uphold what is right. In the spirit realm, the slightest of saints has the authority before God to boldly call for justice through prayer. The conviction power of God is not meant to kill, but to cleanse and to heal. God says in this parable that He is willing to quickly bring justice to answer those who are crying out to Him day and night.

The second principle is seen in the next parable of the Pharisee and the Tax Collector. **(Luke 18:9-14)** Rather than rising up in self-righteousness like the Pharisee, intercessors must remember that they too were once helpless, trapped sinners in need of a Savior. We need to beat our breasts and plead for God's mercy for godless offenders, not look down our nose at society's ills.

Here is an example of the private intercession that can turn the tide of evil. "I heard a story about a man here in the States who had witnessed to his unsaved friend and prayed for him for years. One day, that friend came over to borrow a tool, but no one was home. So he went to the tool shed to find what he was looking for when, suddenly, the Presence of God overtook him. He was convicted of his sins and broke down, putting his faith in Jesus at that very moment. When he told his Christian friend what has happened to him, he found out there was a simple explanation: That faithful believer had prayed with tears for his salvation for a period of years, making intercession for his soul in that very shed. The Holy Spirit was there! Now multiply that picture a thousand times over and spread it across cities, counties, states, and even nations and you have a glorious picture of revival!"[4]

---

4   *Holy Fire*, PP 237,238

Boldness in authority to uphold what is right (justice) combined with humble, heart-felt compassion for lost sinners (mercy) makes for effective intercession by the private assembly. Will we rise up like the Pharisee and say to God, ""I'm glad I'm not like them!" or will we identify with the sins of our nation and pray as if our own personal forgiveness was at stake? Is there enough love in our hearts to cry over the condition of at least one person, forbidding his soul to enter into hell? Private godly sorrow expressed by the saints has effectual influence with God. He will listen and He will visit on behalf of those who cry out to Him day and night and He will bring conviction power with Him when He comes.

TAKE THE LIMITS OFF OF GOD THROUGH
GODLY SORROW!

---

* Do you become grieved over the sin that you see happening around you?
* Are you quick to judge or quick to pray?
* Are you currently praying for the lost?
* Ask God to lead you in a time of godly sorrow and intercession for your neighborhood, city or area.

CHRISTIAN DISCIPLINE

READ GALATIANS 5:16-25

You may know people who have voluntarily joined the Army or Marines in order to buckle down in life and learn discipline. They felt that they could become motivated by forcing themselves to do something hard. Perhaps they wanted a commanding officer to enforce some rules upon them. For whatever reason, they joined the service because they thought it was a good way to counter a weakness that they saw in their own personality.

This scripture passage is a lesson that contrasts the grip of unruly sinful nature versus the disciplined Spirit-filled life. We are to resist the unholy desires of the natural man and voluntarily come under the rule of the Holy Spirit who leads us in the ways of God.

Our weakness of laziness and lack of discipline is a product of our self-life. By nature, we dislike anything that disturbs our own little world that we want for ourselves. We do not welcome responsibility and self-discipline nor do we enjoy putting forth effort for positive moral activity. Instead, our tendency is to be sedentary and self-indulgent. We prefer to be served rather than to serve. And we normally put things off that we are supposed to do rather than plan ahead.

Like those people who join the Army, at some point in life we need to convince ourselves that discipline is something good and necessary that will benefit us. **"He who ignores discipline despises himself, but whoever heeds correction gains understanding."** (Proverbs 15:32 NIV) The definition of discipline is: to train, to prepare, to correct or reprimand, to supervise, govern or keep in line. Some types of discipline include: 1) training, schooling, preparation 2) correction, reprimand, rebuke 3) to preside over, govern, supervise or keep in line. Often, discipline must be carried out by a stronger, more accomplished authority. But the trainee must accept the training being imposed in order for change to occur.

Studies show that only 40 percent of people have strong personal beliefs to which they are committed. (20 percent in one direction and 20 percent in the opposite direction!) That leaves 60 percent of people who are followers and who will be swayed by the bold opinions of the 20 percent who are most vocal.[5] These statistics tell us that the life game-plan for most people is to "go with the flow." They do not question where the "flow" is taking them because they are too weak-willed to step out of the comfort of the crowd.

Christians do not have to be swept along in the multitudes of people going nowhere. If you find yourself lacking strong personal convictions, don't feel bad. The Bible is full of strong assertions about life. We have a God who absolutely loves to train and discipline us for our own good, and is willing to give you all of His opinions as your own! **"My son, do not despise the Lord's discipline and do not resent his rebuke, because the Lord disciplines those he loves, as a Father the son he delights in."** (Proverbs 3:11-12 NIV)

Discipline is the pathway to spiritual growth. We have to put forth time and effort, change our habits and learn new skills in order to manage the grace and opportunities

---

5   *Raising The Standard,* P. 11

for advancement that God wants to give. It is God's will to override our lazy, unruly flesh by the power of His Spirit. He wants to make something of us. We must see the benefit of it so that we will do our part to follow through. If we are not disciplined, we will not fully utilize the power and resources that come to us. The more we exercise our Christian disciplines, the stronger, more clear-minded and steadfast we will become. But we need to want this growth for ourselves.

Passive, careless, uncommitted Christians cannot be used as the driving force that God needs to advance the Gospel and curtail evil. **"From the days of John the Baptist until now, the kingdom of heaven has been forcefully advancing, and forceful men lay hold of it." (Matthew 11:12 NIV)** Perseverance to carry out the will of God is a result of discipline. If we do not hear God well and operate under spiritual principles, then we will miss important strategic callings that we were meant to fulfill. Forceful men lay hold of the kingdom of Heaven only after God fully lays hold of them.

The following is a list of some Christian disciplines and their benefits. These are some methods to train us to be more godly, alert, decisive, dependable and successful:

- Meditation—helps us to think
- Prayer—helps us to focus and communicate
- Fasting—helps us to abstain and gain self-control
- Study—helps us to read and apply
- Submission—helps us to humble ourselves and yield
- Service—helps us to give to others
- Solitude—helps us to be consecrated and undistracted
- Confession—helps us to be truthful
- Worship—helps us to be grateful
- Guidance—helps us to be careful and obedient
- Celebration—helps us to be joyful

The Holy Spirit has an amazing ability to strengthen and stabilize us inwardly through prayer and through the Word of God. He enables us to say "yes" to what is right and "no" to what is wrong, to be able to distinguish the difference, and to speak up for what we have come to believe. God looks ahead in time and sees His people as a vast army recruited through love, trained in the counsel of His Word and strategically positioned to carry out His mission. We can easily be part of that prestigious camp if we will just decide to buckle down and implement the practices of the faith.

TAKE THE LIMITS OFF OF GOD THROUGH CHRISTIAN DISCIPLINE!

---

* Has laziness and lack of motivation been a problem in your life? Do you want to change to become more disciplined?
* List the advantages for you to have greater discipline. Then pray through that list.
* Do you see discipline and correction as good and necessary in living life to its fullest?
* Ask God to challenge you in a practical way.

HARMLESS AS A DOVE

READ EPHESIANS 3: 1-13

When we publicly identify ourselves as Christians, people begin to watch our lives because they expect us to be different. They know that our beliefs should be proven by the way we live. When we live out the commands of Christ, then our claim of knowing God is credible because we act like we do. Our behavior says, "God is real, and He expects me to live by His standards." **"Make every effort to live in peace with all men and to be holy; without holiness no one will see the Lord." (Hebrews 12:14 NIV)**

We need to be careful to maintain a gentle, approachable manner, harmless as a dove, if we hope to share Christ with others. People today carry a tremendous load of guilt and emotional baggage that they quickly share with someone who is willing to listen. We need to be stable, peaceful and calm in our emotions in order to listen and give godly counsel to those the Lord brings to us. God loves it when we are open and available to minister to hurting people. **"...He who loves his fellow man has fulfilled the law...love your neighbor as yourself. Love does no harm to its neighbor. Therefore love is the fulfillment of the law." (Romans 13: 8-10 NIV)**

The Spirit of God seeks the nature of Jesus to descend upon like a dove. The nature of Jesus is **"love, joy, peace,**

patience, kindness, goodness, faithfulness, gentleness and self-control." (Galatians 5:22-23 NIV) We will become attractive to the Spirit when we are harmless to others. **"I want men everywhere to lift up holy hands in prayer, without anger or disputing."** (1 Timothy 2:8 NIV)

People often resort to anger when they are hurt, fearful or don't get their own way. They use anger as a tool to force their way or bring about change. It is extremely selfish to use loud, mean, threatening words against another person. Exhibiting fits of rage will release evil power that can be felt in a person's spirit.

Other harmful behavior habits include sarcasm, mocking, put-downs and accusations. When we act like this, we send a message to others that we are not safe to be around. Like walking "time bombs" waiting to go off, angry people are not easy to be close to because they normally vent at those closest to them.

In reading this scripture passage, we are encouraged to lead a life worthy of the calling we have received. God has chosen each of us to represent Him to others, and we must pay attention to that calling. We have been given the spiritual resources to rid ourselves of selfish, habitual anger and other unloving behavior. We must pray for conviction for God to show us our blind spots of harshness. He will remove the root cause of our anger if we really want it to stop.

The Lord wants prayer to be our sole resource for the help and change we need. Answered prayer will soothe our fears and frustrations. God will be faithful to be mindful of us, but it is our responsibility to be mindful of how we are treating others.

TAKE THE LIMITS OFF OF GOD BY BEING HARMLESS AS A DOVE!

---

* Do you think people expect a higher standard of behavior from you once they learn you are a Christian?
* How do you react when you are hurt, fearful, or don't get your own way?
* Is habitual anger a tool that you use against others?
* Will you renounce this habit and ask God to work His patience and gentleness in you?

REMEMBERING TO SAY "THANKS"

READ LUKE 17: 11-19

Like the mist of a sweetly scented perfume, an attitude of gratefulness filling our lives makes us pleasant and attractive to God. We can learn to be grateful just by observing other people who have this aroma. The Bible gives us accounts of people so that we will draw moral conclusions as we read: "This person did right before God and the others did wrong." These inner conclusions give the Holy Spirit something to get hold of and check us when we find ourselves in similar situations.

In this passage, Jesus makes an example of the thankfulness of the Samaritan. Ten lepers cried out to God for mercy. God answered, and they all gained their lives back from their dread disease. It was lawful for the men to go show themselves to the priest to be declared clean, and so they ran off. But it was love returned that caused one man to come back and thank God. This shows us that Almighty God cannot force us to love Him back. He can only show us an example of the right response to His mercy and hope that we will remember to say, "Thanks!"

Jewish law provided for a "Thank Offering" or a "Fellowship Offering" if a person wanted to express his thankfulness to God. **"These are the regulations for the**

fellowship offering a person may present to the Lord: If he offers it as an expression of thankfulness, then along with this sacrifice of thanksgiving he is to offer cakes of bread made without yeast and mixed with oil…" (Leviticus 7:11-12 NIV) The burnt offering, the grain offering, the sin offering, and the guilt offering were required sacrifices made to God for specific purposes. The Thank Offering was optional—a sacrifice over and above what was required. God knew that when He gave the law, gratefulness could not be legislated. It had to freely flow from each person's will as an expression of returned love.

When the healed Samaritan came back to Jesus, he bowed and worshipped at Jesus' feet, performing in his heart the Thank Offering mentioned in Scripture. The Samaritan was not familiar with Jewish law. Jesus was making the point to the Jews that thankfulness was right by law, but it was even more right by love.

Gratefulness is not only a display of love but also a display of humility. In it we recognize that we don't earn or deserve the mercy and healing that God has lavished upon us. Christ's death on the Cross was a love sacrifice for us. We need to value and appreciate God's loving care of our eternal souls.

An ungrateful attitude truly frustrates the love of God. When His goodness is not appreciated, the atmosphere of praise in which He dwells is stifled. People complain so easily when things don't go their way. Complaints such as "we don't like this and we don't like that!" are grating sounds in God's ear. It implies that God does not meet our expectations and that we are displeased with Him!

Ungratefulness is selfish pride based on the assumption that we have something automatically coming to us. We carry a false expectation and haughtily believe when we receive an item, it was supposed to be ours anyway!

Ungratefulness is unloving because it fails to honor the giver's act of love.

We can never pay back to Jesus what He did for us on the Cross. To try to pay back is ludicrous pride. But when we fill ourselves with appreciation for God, thankfulness and returned love will motivate us to take action. Some final instructions to the church of the Thessalonians: **"Be joyful always; give thanks in all circumstances, for this is God's will for you in Christ Jesus. Do not put out the Spirit's fire..."** **(1 Thessalonians 4:16-22 NIV)** Believers need to personally guard themselves against proud, ungrateful complaining that repels the presence of God in their midst. Instead, be glad that Jesus died for you, and that He continues to be a good, giving God. Give that free-will Thank Offering upon the altar of your heart not only because it fulfills God's requirement but because you truly want to.

TAKE THE LIMITS OFF OF GOD BY REMEMBERING
TO SAY "THANKS!"

---

* Think about how God has shown His mercy and goodness towards you.
* Do you remember to thank Him for all He has done and is doing?
* What is your attitude towards people who have helped you?
* What do you generally vocalize daily—complaining or gratefulness?

SEXUAL PURITY

READ 1 CORINTHIANS 6:12-20

There are many topics in the Bible that require additional prayer and study to gain understanding of God's revealed will. Sexual purity, though, is not one of those topics. God's will concerning human sexuality could not be any clearer to us. Twelve of the 26 books in the New Testament discuss this subject openly and bluntly. Any Christian who reads the Bible or sits under Bible teaching has no excuse for not realizing God's requirement for sexual purity. Let me state it simply here: it is God's will that all sexual relations are reserved for men and women who are married. Marriage is between one man and one woman, and married couples should stay faithful to each other. PERIOD! Any activity that deviates from this standard is perverse, self-seeking and abhorrent to the Holy Spirit. Don't bother asking God to bless anything that is against His will.

There is no question that our society has accepted immorality in the name of "romance" and "love," re-naming lust and pretending that its motives are honorable. There seems to be no end of sex scenes played out before our eyes on television or in movies. As a nation, our increased appetite for sensuality has had a plummeting affect on moral decency. The devil knows that the way back to innocence is a long, hard road.

But God's Word does not bow to current moral sub-standards. The Church is not to be polluted with sexual immorality the same way that society is. The Bible even goes so far as to warn believers not to even associate with those who call themselves Christians and yet remain sexually impure. **"But now I am writing you that you must not associate with anyone who calls himself a brother but is sexually immoral..."** (**1 Corinthians 5:11 NIV**)

I remember a time when a woman from the church called me to ask me to alter her daughter's dress for her upcoming wedding. When I called the daughter, it became clear that she was already living with her fiancé. I turned down the sewing job as God told me not to help her because He was so opposed to her living arrangements. This was not the only instance of immorality I've encountered with Christians. In fact, I come across couples compromising in this area quite often in the Church. We need to know that turning on to lust is an absolute turn off to the Spirit of God! New Testament writers were well aware of this and were cautious to preserve the presence of God in their midst rather than condescend to immoral believers.

The reason why God is so opposed to this type of sin is because human sexuality is a physical representation of the oneness and intimacy that God achieves through the indwelling Holy Spirit in the believer. He is our spiritual "Lover." God's union with man through Christ is a holy, pure and unique relationship. God made it possible for a measure of Himself to be deposited in the heart of every believer, and we are to hold this presence sacred, near and dear.

God also glorifies himself through the covenant of marriage. The holy union of man and woman mirrors God's loving commitment to mankind. When the model of His love relationship with man is perverted by selfishness, God is dishonored. The Bible makes it clear in our passage that no other sin dishonors God so grossly than the misuse of our own bodies through immorality. **"The body is not meant for sexual immorality, but for the Lord, and the Lord for the body."** **(1 Corinthians 6:13 NIV)** When people do this, they are refusing God's control over their physical bodies and allowing their own desires to rule them. Illicit sex becomes the "god" they seek and serve.

We are not to make the same mistakes as Esau, who for a single meal gave up his inheritance. **(Hebrews 12:16)** In other words, don't pass up the spiritual benefits of the kingdom that God has for you just to enjoy momentary pleasure for yourself now. If you are single, take heart in knowing that, although sexual desire is very strong when stirred up, God has greater power to stop you from giving in. If you are married, do not ruin your life and the lives of your family by acting treacherously through adultery. God has a way of reasoning with us to cool off those heated desires to help us re-focus.

Most importantly, the Holy Spirit is tremendously released in the lives of believers who strictly adhere to God's standard of purity, not even allowing a hint of immortality to cloud their life and offend God. The purity of the thoughts of our heart will attract our soul's Lover to meet us in all our needs. Take comfort. God knows all about real love...because God IS love.

TAKE THE LIMITS OFF OF GOD
THROUGH SEXUAL PURITY!

---

*   Whether single or married, what situations are you in that have the potential for sexual temptation?

*   Are you convinced that any hint of immorality is wrong before God?
*   Will you trust God to remove you from any immoral relationship and help you to live in a manner that glorifies Him?
*   Will you pray and ask Him for power to resist any subtle temptation even if you have remained pure and faithful?

FAITH NEEDS FEET

READ JOSHUA 3: 9-17

The expression "talk is cheap" conveys an important spiritual principle that true faith will produce life action. The Bible instructs us not just to read its message, but to use its important truths for daily living. Without personal practice, the teachings of the Bible remain mere lofty ideals painting pictures of a better world. **"Show me your faith without deeds, and I will show you my faith by what I do." (James 2:18 NIV)** The writer argues that our actions based on our belief is the only real evidence that we truly believe. Performance proves that we have made that ideal our very own.

Action that is taken because of a heart-held conviction is called "a step of faith." Just as He did in our passage, God watches to act upon what we truly believe and responds to prove His Word. **"Come here and listen to the words of the Lord your God." (vs 9)** If we want to stir up God's Spirit to move on our behalf, we first have to get moving and put some feet to our faith!

Christians need to position themselves (with their feet!) to be of practical help to others (as evidence of their faith!) as God leads. To be useful and effective, we must pay attention to both the spiritual and the practical sides of ministry. We operate between two worlds, the spiritual and the material, and must wisely balance our participation in both.

For example, we should possess a fiery passion for the cause of Christ by doing things that are seemingly foolish, yet we must also draw upon sound reasoning. We are called to self-sacrifice as a higher way to live, but we must use discernment as to how much we are supposed to do for people. On one hand we must constantly give ourselves to prayer, yet physical work must also be done. We receive guidance from God's holy Word, yet we must know how to operate in the world system. Lastly, we enter into a loving, uplifting union with God, yet our hardest lessons come from learning to forgive, be patient and hope for the best in people. From these examples, we can see that believing is the easy part. Carrying out that belief is the challenge!

In our passage, God proved several things to Joshua and all of Israel as they dared to step foot into the flooded Jordan:

1) God's will is important to God. He has a goal, a plan, a purpose for everything He tells us to do. When we cooperate, He will be responsible to carry out His will through us.

2) God is sovereign over the material realm. A word from Him—and all nature must obey! He will work out the physical details as we travel in His plan.

3) The ark represents the presence of the Lord. As believers, we carry the presence of the Lord inside of us. God is very attentive to His Spirit. Therefore, we should never accuse the Lord of neglecting or abandoning us because that is impossible.

4) We must have faith in God to the degree that we believe what He tells us in spite of what we see happening around us. God's Word should become our true reality.

As the priests stepped into the Jordan with the ark lifted upon their shoulders, the waters receded and piled straight up into a wall of water around them! This spectacle is no less true for us. When we begin to step out and live by faith, circumstances will build up against us. Our vulnerability is then seen by onlookers against the backdrop of God's staying power. If we refuse to fear, our continued faith will see us safely to the other side. People will invariably admit that we could never have accomplished what we did without God's assistance. God promises that He will use our steps of faith to show the world that He is real and that He is with us.

TAKE THE LIMITS OFF OF GOD BY PUTTING
FEET TO OUR FAITH!

---

* Truthfully evaluate yourself. Are you a "talker" or a "doer"?
* What has God shown you that He wants you to do?
* Have you responded with fear or with faith?
* Are you willing to advance to greater levels of trust in Christ? Will you put "feet to your faith?

SIN IS SERIOUS

READ LUKE 15: 11-24

Sin doesn't seem too serious once you have it as part of your life. Anything can seem normal if you do it long enough. As an example, an article in the paper gave some recipes for preparing locusts as a side dish for a meal. While the insects are still fresh from the tree, snip off the wings and the legs; then boil one cup of locust bodies in two quarts of water for 12 minutes. Salt to taste or add your favorite salsa!

What may seem disgustingly abhorrent in America is a tasty delicacy in Japan! Food preferences are determined by our cultural upbringing. The same principle applies to sin. Our tolerance level is determined by the cultural influences that people become used to. The declining moral standards we see have become normal to us and therefore acceptable.

In the parable of the lost son, the young man must have been living out a strong fantasy in his mind for him to ask for his inheritance, implying that things would be better for him if his father were dead! Dreams of what the world can offer us if we only had the money is a very common yearning in people. It makes people dissatisfied with the life they are living. They think they are missing out on something more exciting. I think that selfish fantasy dreams like this cause marriage problems for people always wondering if the "grass is greener" with someone else.

The father obliged the son's request and watched the son head off to a far away land. After awhile the son's fantasy of living off his wealth did not come true and he had to go out and find a job. The opportunities were not as plentiful as he imagined, so he had to take whatever job he could find. He was forced out of his fantasy when the reality of starvation finally got his attention. Like waking up from a dream, the Bible says, **"he came to his senses."** **(vs 17)**

The turning point for the young man came when he not only hated what he was doing to himself, he also hated what he was doing against his family and against God. He finally realized the seriousness of his own sin and how it had ruined him.

There are two lies that often undermine this important realization and can block our renunciation of sinful habits. The first lie says, "It's not really that bad!" This reasoning minimizes the true weight of sin. It reduces the trespass down to a minor infraction that can be overlooked. No need for alarm! No real harm done!

The second lie is, "I can handle it!" We don't believe there will be consequences for what we are doing wrong and if there are, we are slick enough to get ourselves out of trouble. We see ourselves as somewhat "bullet-proof!"

This reasoning does not take into account the power of supernatural evil that is on the other side of sin's pleasure! This assumption is very foolish and dangerous. We need to get one thing straight, we cannot handle supernatural evil. Only Christ can handle it for us. The forces behind sin are nothing to play with. We should have a healthy respect for evil power yet not fear it. Christ must battle the devil for us.

The lost son came to a full realization of his wrong thinking. First he realized his sin was an offense against himself. Sin has a degrading effect on people. It causes us to live lower than we should, bringing on feelings of worthlessness, shame and guilt. **"I am no longer worthy to be called your son." (vs 19)**

Next, his sin was an offense against his family. We must realize what we are doing to other people when we live wrongly. Many lives are touched by the ripple effect of sin. Think of mothers who grieve over wayward children or parents who disregard their responsibility to love and nurture their own children. A family member can be out having a gay old time in sin while the family suffers intensely.

Last, the son realized that his sin was against God. **"I have sinned against heaven..." (vs 18)** This is the most important awakening we can have. We hurt God by our sin because he sees the full spiritual spectrum of our choices. Like the father in the parable, He lets us make our mistakes, but He hates seeing us hurt ourselves, our family or miss out on His best that He had waiting for us. I have seen Christians who wanted to serve God in a greater way be disqualified or bypassed because of favorite sin issues they would not give up.

The response of the father in this story shows the true forgiving heart of God the Father. God wants each of His children to be secure in His love and acceptance of them. God is willing to work with us to bring us out of sin habits if we are willing to face some serious realizations. He knows that the clean-up process is gradual. He also wants us to be challenged in our spiritual life so that our Christian walk is exciting enough that we won't long for the excitement of the world. We become self-assured when we know we are involved in important work for the greatest cause on earth. God also wants us to walk upright before Him and have a healthy self-respect, dignity and pride. This way we will shun dirty, degrading activities that threaten to spoil our lives.

The Holy Spirit is at work to separate us from the things that cause sin. This work of separation helps us to see the seriousness of sin from God's viewpoint. Heaven still rejoices when sinners repent! God wants to bring us to our senses more and more to see the awfulness of sin as He sees it.

TAKE THE LIMITS OFF OF GOD BY
SEEING SIN AS SERIOUS!

---

* What influences in society have an influence in your home?
* Do you understand how sin affects others?
* What things have affected your family members?
* Do you understand that personal sin is not a light issue?

CONSIDERING GOD'S GOODNESS

READ PSALM 107: 1-43

"Why do you call me good?" Jesus immediately qualified the rich young ruler's address of Him as "good teacher." **"Jesus answered, 'No one is good—except God alone.'"** **(Mark 10: 18 NIV)** Jesus sensed that the young man's faith was in his own righteousness. In one sentence, Jesus discredited the saving ability of man's goodness and established that God was distinctly good, unmatched by human goodness and therefore the only true good. If the inquirer really wanted eternal life then he would have to admit to goodness that he was incapable of that was far beyond himself.

It is important for our emotional well-being to believe that God is good, that He is merciful and that He wants the best for us. **"The Lord is good to all; he has compassion on all he has made." (Psalm 145:9 NIV)** People will despair if they are without hope. But if they know that God is good, then that belief will carry them.

During this hour of grace, God's temperament towards mankind is still benevolent, kind, gracious, generous, humane, tender-hearted and willing to help. He not only has the ability but also the inclination to relieve and save. But, like the rich young ruler, God is not opposed to allowing circumstances to arise that force us to look beyond self and consider God's goodness. It is never pleasant when God empties us and brings us to a point of admitting the lack of our own abilities. Sometimes we are backed into a corner and can see no answers, no power, and no control coming from ourselves. That is the time we can cry out to the Lord because we believe in His goodness.

Our passage describes many of these situations and how God graciously answered. For example, some **"wandered in desert wastelands" (vs 4)** Confusion and lack of direction in life is a common problem with people. We must connect with God in order to find out our purpose in life. Otherwise, we wander aimlessly, never knowing what we are supposed to do with ourselves.

Others **"sat in darkness and in gloom...for they had rebelled against the words of God." (vs 10)** This suggests the emotional disorders, even depression that rebellion brings. When we follow our own feelings rather than the Word of God, we become unhappy prisoners of our own conclusions. But if we cry out to the Lord, He will show us the error in our thinking and the troubles of our soul, and will bring us out of sadness and despair.

Others **"suffered affliction because of their iniquities." (vs 17)** Most of the time, we can only blame ourselves for the hard times we are having. We are experts at doing bad things for ourselves. We cling to destructive addictions such as drinking, smoking, over-eating and neglect of physical needs such as good nutrition, rest and exercise. The body can only take so much abuse before it starts to break down. Yet if we cry out to the Lord, He will save us from chronic bad habits that harm us.

The next account describes a storm at sea that sends the ship out of control. Life is full of unexpected trouble. When disaster strikes, we stagger like drunkards from upset and loss. But if we cry to the Lord, He will steady us and at least give us a sense of His presence through the storm. At the end, we have an inner peace from trusting Him rather than become overwhelmed with fear.

Lastly, for others **"he turns a desert into pools of water, a parched land into springs of water."** **(vs 33)** This speaks of spiritually dry periods when we don't sense God because His presence seems far from us. We become desperately thirsty to "drink" from the flow of His Spirit. Again, if we cry out for this need, He will bless with His presence and even bring a spiritual increase that we will recognize.

If you identify with any of these examples, then it is time to cry out to the Lord because you believe in His goodness. Many times people react to difficulties by looking around and becoming angry with others who don't seem to be going through as much. Instead of hoping in God's goodness for themselves, they jealously hate others for their presumed comfort. Envy is the selfish assumption that someone else has it easier or better than you do. There is nothing that binds up help and relief from God as much as envious resentment of others.

I have seen many reactions of envy and selfish hating among church members. Covetousness is the feeling of resentment we have towards others because they have something that we want for ourselves. Some common examples include: hating someone for how good they look, how much money they seem to have, their expensive home, their spouse, children or family, their position in ministry, or their giftedness.

People bind up and spoil their own answers from God with their angry reactions and jealous attitudes against others. **"And without faith it is impossible to please God, because anyone who comes to him must believe he exists and that he rewards those who earnestly seek him."** **(Hebrews 11:6 NIV)** Belief in God's existence is incomplete faith.

This verse says that we must also believe the truth about His good nature and that He will honor our faith by a display of His goodness. Not only is God real, He is good and He is good to me!

During those times when we are in need, pain, depression or trouble, our response must be to look to God's goodness. Appeal to His mercy, cry out to Him for help and relief. Perhaps we need to do this for an extended period of time. God may be emptying you out of yourself. You still need to believe that God's goodness is beyond all we could ask or imagine. Wait on Him, expecting Him to extend His goodness into your personal circumstances. When His answer comes, the truth will be branded into our memory that God alone is good.

TAKE THE LIMITS OFF OF GOD BY
CONSIDERING GOD'S GOODNESS!

---

* Do you identify with any of these circumstances in this passage?
* Have you learned to cry out to the Lord?
* How do you react when you see others do well or prosper?
* Take a moment to reflect on God's goodness and pray that you would believe rightly about God's character.

CHEERFUL GIVING

READ 2 CORINTHIANS 8:1-15

"It is more blessed to give than to receive." (Acts 20:35) This short straight-forward axiom has the potential to lift people out of their grudging instincts to a higher plane of living. Most parents agree that giving is a key element to harmony in the home and so they teach young children to share. Normally they only teach them the basics, taking this lesson far enough for siblings to get along.

God wants to take His people into a much deeper understanding of His fatherhood which is evidenced through His giving nature. He also wants us to experience the happiness that unselfish giving offers. But first we must give up control of our possessions because we usually stop far short of what we can give by grace.

Practically speaking, Christian ministry requires time, money and resources. Expenses are incurred in the work of communicating the Gospel. God's work can be delayed if resources are not made available by generous giving.

We also may become aware of needs among people we know. We are not supposed to say to people, "I'm praying for you! Hope things get better for you!" and not get involved to some degree to help them. Showing mercy not only extends the love of Christ but also removes the hardness from our own hearts.

In our text, Paul gives an impressive example of generosity in the Macedonian churches and then urges the Corinthians to also **"excel in the grace of giving."** **(vs 7)** Those early believers learned a secret ingredient of brotherhood that bound them together under severe trials. Unusual kindness made Christians distinct among their pagan neighbors. Their love for one another was obvious through giving. As a result, Christianity spread quickly because people saw that it was a better, higher lifestyle and they wanted it for themselves. "The practical expression of Christian love was probably among the most powerful causes of Christian success. Tertullian tells us that the pagans remarked, "See how the Christians love one another."[6] **"Each man should give what he has decided in his heart to give, not reluctantly or under compulsion, for God loves a cheerful giver."** **(2 Corinthians 9:7 NIV)** This verse says that God finds pleasure in people who enjoy giving. We need to give God His good pleasure! I believe there are six main reasons why God loves cheerful giving:

1) Our giving reflects His giving nature. **"Freely you have received, freely give."** **(Matthew 10:8)**
2) The grace of giving conquers our selfish nature. **"Above all, love each other deeply, because love covers over a multitude of sins."** **(1 Peter 4:8)**
3) It is evidence that we are not living for the pleasures of the world but seeking to make an investment in eternity. **"Instead, they were longing for a better country—a heavenly one."** **(Hebrews 11:16)**
4) Cheerful givers are easy, willing vessels in God's hand to touch human hearts, convincing people that God exists and cares. **"I led them with cords of human kindness, with ties of love."** **(Hosea 11:4)**

---

6   *Church History,* P. 228

5) Because the spirit behind cheerful giving is love, this creates a suitable atmosphere for the Holy Spirit to work. **"God is love."** (1 John 4:16)

6) Cheerful giving insures that people are cared for. A family atmosphere is so important for the Church. It is not a business, nor an organization, nor a stage for personal fame. It should be no less than a functional, loving, caring family that acts as a refuge for people in the world to come and be loved. **"A new command I give you: love one another. As I have loved you, so you must love one another. All men will know that you are my disciples if you love one another."** (John 13: 34-35)

If you do not have the faith to give as these verses suggest, then be encouraged that you can grow in giving until it becomes a pleasure to you. Some practical guidelines for giving include:

1) Learn to be happy with what you have and suppress the selfish wanting for more, more, more.

2) Trust God with your finances in the discipline of tithing.

3) Money, possessions, time and services can all be part of your sharing.

4) Don't see God as a "slot-machine god" assuming that if we give then we will get. The scripture **"Give and it will be given to you."** (Matthew 6:38) is meant to change our nature, not to learn a trick for getting. Jesus was saying that our willingness to give will be seen by God and He will consider our hearts as He blesses.

Getting involved with people as needs arise will make our portion of the world a better place. There is a great deal of spiritual light that is spread when we obey the Spirit as he prompts us to give. God will multiply our efforts and will bring much good from the resources we have given in His name. God says to just try Him to see if this principle is true!

TAKE THE LIMITS OFF OF GOD
THROUGH CHEERFUL GIVING!

---

* Growing up, did your parents insist that you share or were you indulged as a child?
* What are your feelings about giving now?
* Do you honor God through tithing?
* Do you see the value in laying up treasures in Heaven now through giving?

RIDDING OURSELVES OF REBELLION

READ ROMANS 13:1-10

Along the Lake Erie shoreline near Cleveland, Ohio break walls have been built to protect lakefront property from being washed away by the endless pounding waves. Similar to the damage done by those waves, the stormy waters of rebellion have risen and washed over our culture, eroding the basic standards of how we should respond to authority. The break walls that the Bible could have built in our society are almost gone. It is not unusual to see people acting disrespectful if not defiant against those over them. Parents, teachers, bosses and government officials are all at a loss at how to deal with rebellious attitudes aimed to defy their leadership.

It becomes the responsibility of the Church to model respect for authority and show that it is the successful way to live. According to our verse, God has chosen to work through the ranks of society to restrain, correct or bless us. Given authorities don't have to be perfect (and probably aren't!) to be God's channel of protection and blessing. God is not a magic genie making things vaporize before us. Instead, He uses the order of society and human relationships to deliver our blessing.

The rebellious do not fully enjoy the benefits of God, though. They cut themselves off by their own hardness of heart. **"The rebellious live in a parched land." (Psalm 68:6 NIV)** For example, if someone has a horrible attitude towards his boss at work, that boss will remember how difficult that employee was to work with all year, bucking every decision, and will offer the promotion to someone else in the department who had a more willing attitude. Or say a husband has a tender hearted moment towards his wife during the day and stops on the way home to buy her flowers. But when he gets home, she has had a rough day with the kids and decides let him have it about the things she is unhappy about! Those flowers may wind up in the trash rather than reward her attitude. These are just a few examples of how we hinder our own progress and blessing with rebellion.

The attitude of rebellion is supported by two wrong underlying assumptions:

1) It is a staunch defense of our personal rights thinking "No one has the right to tell ME what to do!"
2) It is in defense of self-interest which says, "I know how to run my own life!"

As Christians, we have no excuse to hold on to these false assumptions. Having a personal relationship with God through Christ is the foundation of accepting God as our Creator. Because He is God, He has the right to tell us what to do. He will also assign us a human agent to tell us what to do. The Bible says that we are to accept the human authority over us as being sent from God. **"Submit yourselves for the Lord's sake to every authority instituted among men: whether to the king, as the supreme authority, or to the governors, who are sent to him to punish those who do wrong and commend those who do right." (1 Peter 2: 13-14 NIV)**

The Bible also makes it clear that we do not know how to run our own life without God's guidance either. **"As for you, you were dead in your transgressions and sins, in which you used to live when you followed the ways of this world and the ruler of the kingdom of the air, the spirit who is now at work in those who are disobedient." (Ephesians 2:1-2 NIV)**

Rebellion is a product of our own thinking by wanting our own way and then defiantly resisting those who would try to restrain us. Stubbornness keeps habitual rebellion patterns in place. Rebellious people are often angry, resentful, touchy "know-it-alls" who flatly refuse advice from others. These hardened attitudes cut people off from God's sound reasoning and lives are spoiled needlessly.

The key to healing the attitude of "I won't" into "I will!" is to believe the truth of God's Word over your own personal experience with authority figures. If you have resorted to rebellion due to harsh, unfair authority in your past and have lost the willingness to trust people, then you need to place your trust fully in God. He will never disappoint you. You must say to yourself, "Despite my experience, the Bible tells me that authority has been given by God for my good. Therefore, that is the view I will have!"

Here are some suggested practices to work out of rebellious thinking:

1) Make yourself submit. Listen to the directive you have been given and just do it!
2) Honor and respect your authorities. This doesn't mean you have to like them. If you can't respect the person, then respect the position the person holds.
3) Pray for those in authority over you. They are not perfect. Anyone in leadership needs prayer to walk

in God's will instead of his own. God has power to change, strengthen or even replace those who govern us.

God's use of given authority on earth is to train us to become His obedient servants. Once we are trained in obedience, we can enjoy carrying out God's orders because we no longer resent His direct commands. **"No discipline seems pleasant at the time, but painful. Later on, however, it produces a harvest of righteousness and peace for those who have been trained by it." (Hebrews 12:11 NIV)**
Opportunities to do greater levels of ministry will open up for us once we show that we are team players and have the humility to do as we are told by those in charge. The best thing we can do is to learn to value authority and see how it is good for people to fall in line. We will receive the blessing of our obedience as we respect those God has placed over us. And God is glorified when His people are conscious of His supreme rule and choose to live that way!

TAKE THE LIMITS OFF OF GOD
BY RIDDING OURSELVES OF REBELLION!

---

* Do you bristle when someone directly tells you to do something?
* What is your inner thought process when this happens?
* Will you believe what the Bible says about God's intention for the common good through given authority?
* What ways do you need to submit and show more respect to those in authority over you?

SACRIFICIAL LIVING

READ MARK 14: 1-9

American manufacturers work to anticipate their customer's next demand for ease and comfort in our convenience-oriented society. We push a button in the car and the windows go up and down for us. We push another button and the garage door automatically goes up. Then we get inside the house, pull out a frozen dinner, push another button and dinner is on the table! We find more and more ways to cut back on personal effort. The sway of modern marketing is proof that the whim of self nature is to try to always make things easier for ourselves.

I am not complaining about modern conveniences, mind you. I enjoy my air-conditioning and electric lights! But the character building that comes from having to push ourselves to do something hard evaporates when we insist on instant relief.

It is important to remind ourselves that the Christian life revolves around a sacrifice. The sacrificial death of Jesus for the sake of mankind is the pivotal event that gives all meaning to our faith. Our new life in Christ is due to a sacrifice, and that sacrifice was not an easy one. **"He withdrew about a stone's throw beyond them, knelt down and prayed, 'Father, if you are willing, take this cup from me; yet not my will, but yours be done.' An angel from heaven appeared to him and strengthened him. And being in anguish, he prayed**

more earnestly, and his sweat was like drops of blood falling to the ground." (Luke 22: 41-44 NIV) At Gethsemane, the blood sacrifice of the Lamb of God had already begun. Self-nature was condemned at the Cross and the higher nature of self-sacrifice was lifted up and accepted by God. The life and death of Jesus established the way that man should live.

As followers, we must understand that sacrificial living is a foundational theme of our faith. God chooses to make demands on our lives for the saving benefit of others. He sovereignly encroaches on our plans and pleasures in order to seek and save those who are lost.

For example, years ago as a youth leader I counseled a young woman who was suicidal. That was a very costly relationship for me because I spent hours on the phone listening and talking to her along with hours in prayer heading off the enemy's attacks on her life. Today she is a vivacious, dedicated Christian who has inspired many. The world would not have been the same without her. I also refer back to that time as the training ground for other mentoring that I have done.

This theme of sacrificial living is repeated many times in scripture. In our passage, the woman broke open a jar of expensive perfume and poured it out on Jesus' head. **"She poured perfume on my body beforehand to prepare for my burial."** (vs 8) Her act of sacrifice echoed the sacrifice that Christ knew He was going to make. This seemed like a foolish waste to the men watching her. They did not have the spiritual insight to know that extravagant love needs to be answered with extravagant love! Jesus defended her because He knew she understood Him as Savior.

There are several reasons why our lives are like a precious perfume when they are poured out for the sake of others:

1) It mirrors and thereby glorifies the highest sacrifice made by the Son of God

2) The principle of multiplication is activated when we die to self. **"Unless a kernel of wheat falls to the ground and dies, it remains only a single seed. But if it dies, it produces many seeds."** (John 12: 24)

3) Self-sacrifice for the sake of others is the highest act of love and creates an atmosphere for the Holy Spirit to be present. **"Greater love has no one than this, that one lay down his life for his friends."** (John 15:13 NIV)

4) Sacrificial living is a grateful love offering given back to Christ. He gave us His all and we owe Him everything. **"Therefore, I urge you brothers, in view of God's mercy, to offer your bodies as living sacrifices, holy and pleasing to God—which is your spiritual worship."** (Romans 12: 1 NIV)

As "living sacrifices" our plans for our own life go up in smoke as God changes our agenda to His. This is not an easy doctrine nor a pleasant one. To go against the very grain of self for the sake of Christ is a severe test of our love for God. But God does not ignore our sacrifice nor take it lightly. He delights in costly faith. **"Precious in the sight of the Lord is the death of his saints."** (Psalm 116:15 NIV) He knows that we are using the one and only life we will have for Him. This is sweet and welcome perfume for our exalted Head and there is a beauty about this lifestyle that Christ absolutely adores. **"She has done a beautiful thing to me."** (vs 6) Jesus will continue to defend and respond to this form of active worship of Him.

TAKE THE LIMITS OFF OF GOD
THROUGH SACRIFICAL LIVING!

---

* Do you understand the sacrifice that was made for you by Christ? How has it impacted you?
* Why would self-sacrifice be more loving than self-indulgence?
* Are you afraid to get involved with people because of what that involvement might cost you?
* Are you willing to abandon your dreams, pleasures and plans on the altar and allow God to use you as He pleases?

QUESTIONING OUR OWN THINKING

READ EPHESIANS 4: 17-24

"Diane, why are you being shy?" The Holy Spirit came to me while I was walking to the mailbox to pay my monthly bills. I wasn't expecting a deep discussion about the essence of my personality. My mind was still preoccupied with the sudden evaporation of my checking account! But I quickly switched gears and listened to His reasoning.

"Do you know where shyness comes from?"

"Yes, Lord, it has its roots in self and is a result of shame and the fear of man." I knew enough of the proper theology to recite it back.

"Don't you need people?"

"Oh, yes Lord, when I close myself off from people I feel terribly lonely!"

"Don't you want to introduce people to the Gospel?"

"Oh, yessss Lord, that is my number one goal in life!

"Then why are you doing it?

Silence. I didn't know why I was doing it. All I could think of was that I had always been that way. Now God was calling that habit into question. The thought of living without that relational crutch was scary for me. But just because I couldn't imagine myself not being shy didn't make it impossible for me to live differently. I believed that if God wanted to change something about my personality He certainly could.

So on my way back from the mailbox, I decided I wasn't going to be shy anymore! God had set me free from an emotional trap just by making me question my own thinking. I saw that I was holding myself back with shyness, but more importantly I was holding God back as well.

This verse gives us a before and after description of our thinking patterns once we are in Christ. The key to Christlikeness is the continual questioning of our thinking once we realize that our old thought patterns are no good. The Bible describes our old ways of thinking as futile. (**vs 17**) Futile means: useless, empty, hollow, worthless, petty and trivial. When we see Christ as the center of all, we need to re-evaluate our thinking so that we will think as Christ thinks.

This is hard medicine for some people because their mind is like a "god" to them. **"Because your heart is proud and you have said, 'I am a god; I sit in the seat of the gods, in the heart of the seas'; Yet you are a mortal, and no god, though you compare your mind with the mind of a god.'"** (**Ezekiel 28: 2 NIV**) Before people know Christ, they live by desires that originate in their minds. With no voice other than their own, their thoughts become their ruling force—right or wrong.

Sin clouds our viewpoint. In it we do not have a right understanding of God, ourselves or others. Our thoughts are grossly distorted by the way sin has compelled us to believe. Our minds are loaded with selfish pride. We are so very pleased with ourselves by how much we know. Recently at a birthday party I met a husband who told me that his "goal" in life was to change his wife to make her into the kind of person he felt she should be! He chuckled in his pride after his remark. From his actions toward her, I could see that he had it very strongly in his mind to exert fierce control over her life to feel powerful. I knew that his "goal" was not of God but from himself. Christ's glory in that home will be stunted as long as that husband focuses on changing his wife and not himself.

There are many other corrupted thinking patterns that people operate in. Here are some common examples:

1) "I am the only one suffering!" Self pity robs us of our courage to go on. "Poor me!" is the thinking pattern that the devil uses to magnify our troubles and take us into hopelessness.

2) "Other people are doing things purposely against me!" The spirit of offense speaks to us, convincing us that we are helpless victims. We become suspicious and untrusting of others. We also ignore our part in the offense.

3) "Other people are stupid!" Haughty contempt causes us to look down on others, deeming them beneath us in intelligence. We don't honor the value of other human beings.

4) "I would never do anything like that!" A self-righteous spirit underestimates the potential for depravity that is in all of us and refuses to accept our capability of doing wrong.

These are just some of the thoughts that God wants to call into question. God knows that if we agree with Him enough to change our thinking then a change will occur in our life. Here is the key: just because we can't imagine something differently doesn't mean that God can't change it! We limit God by putting a ceiling on Him with our own imaginations. We cannot know or imagine all that God can do. **"Now to him who is able to do immeasurably more that all we ask or imagine..." (Ephesians 3:20 NIV)**

The **"new self created to be like God in true righteous-ness and holiness" (vs 24)** is the right goal for the redeemed of God to have. God gives us a wonderful second chance in Christ to live right before Him. If we make up our minds to stop holding Him back, He will pull us out of the ruts of thinking that we have created in our minds.

TAKE THE LIMITS OFF OF GOD BY
QUESTIONING OUR OWN THINKING!

---

* Name some old thinking patterns that you know need to be changed.
* What are some "quirks" in your personality that may be holding you back?
* Can you imagine yourself behaving differently? If not, are you willing to believe God anyway?
* Ask God to show your thought patterns from the old self. Ask Him to tear down those strongholds of selfish pride that keep you from changing your mind.

THE POWER OF THE CROSS

READ LEVITICUS 14: 48-53

The millennium celebration of the year 2000 we watched via international broadcast was a once in a lifetime event and truly a milestone in human history. Yet with all the fireworks, parades and extravaganzas, the world woke up in their respective time zones virtually unchanged. Why? Although January 1, 2000 was an amazing event, there was no inherent power in it. Not so with the Cross!

The Cross—or more specifically the spiritual feat performed by God to break the power of sin through the death of His Son—has profound, unique, significant power that is fully available for mankind today. Our verse in Leviticus gives us a simple, yet complete picture of the spiritual work of the Cross.

In the Old Testament, leprosy was a dreaded disease that was given much instruction by the Law of Moses on how to deal with it. Because it was so contagious, an infected person had to be banished from the camp, his clothes and housing properly disposed of. This is God's picture of sin, the inner disease that should be highly feared, loathed and not loved as part of our life.

This scripture describes the rite that was performed if a leprous mildew was found on the house walls, plastered over, and did not return. The home was pronounced clean after this ceremony. Two birds were chosen for this rite of cleansing. One was killed while the live bird was dipped in the blood and with fresh water. This is a picture of the atonement of Christ. His life was taken as satisfactory payment of the debt that the moral crime of sin incurred against God.

After sprinkling the house with blood and fresh water, the live bird was released into an open field. This act pictures our purification from sin. It represents the emotionally free, whole, unhindered life that we can enjoy as God removes the damage of sin from our lives. These two works of the Cross are mentioned in this verse: **"It teaches us to say "No" to ungodliness and worldly passions, and to live self controlled, upright and godly lives in this present age, while we wait for the blessed hope—the glorious appearing of our great God and Savior, Jesus Christ, who gave himself for us to redeem us from all wickedness and to purify for himself a people that are his very own, eager to do what is good."** (Titus 2:12-14 NIV)

There are two distinct works of the Cross that continue to be available to us. The first is redemption. Through the atonement, Christ brings us back into right relationship with God. The second is purification. This is the ongoing process of removing the affects of sin, keeping us in right fellowship with God.

The supernatural provision of the Cross is a fact. God made it possible for our sin to be forgiven by grace by just believing and receiving. What God did for us through Jesus we could not have done for ourselves. **"This righteousness from God comes through faith in Jesus Christ to all who believe. There is no difference, for all have sinned and**

fall short of the glory of God, and are justified freely by his grace...God presented him as a sacrifice of atonement, through faith in his blood." (Romans 3: 22-25 NIV)

There is also power in the Cross. In 2,000 years it remains perfect in its power. There has been no power lost, it just needs to be accessed. For example, if a town had only one ATM machine to use over the weekend, that limited storehouse of cash would be used up by Saturday night and people's needs would go unmet. But the Cross has unlimited access and unlimited power on our behalf. As many as are willing to receive Christ can have Him and those who have Him will be able to be purified as much as they want. It gives God good pleasure when people take advantage of the power of the Cross that He so willingly provided.

The key issue is our participation in the Cross. We must personally understand our leprous condition and see our need of a Savior. We may dip again and again into those cleansing waters of forgiveness, accessing the power of the Cross and experience freedom. Through redemption and sanctification, Christ made the provision of our eternal happiness and also our internal happiness. We just need to go to Him to participate in this power.

TAKE THE LIMITS OFF OF GOD THROUGH
THE POWER OF THE CROSS!

---

* Do you understand that, through the atonement, Christ accomplished for you a righteousness that you could not have for yourself?

* Understanding this foundational truth, will you fully receive the benefits of the Cross that Christ purchased for you?
* Will you allow God to do a work of sanctification in you?
* Thank Him for His sacrificial provision and ask Him to help you access the power of the Cross in a greater way.

SEEING CHRIST AS OUR ONLY ANSWER

READ 1 SAMUEL 1:1-20

Our faith should rest in God's power alone. Many times we see Him as a "last resort" rather than our only possible way. Hannah suffered from pressure on all sides. In that society, barrenness was considered to be a disgrace. Her husband's second wife mocked and chided her, making her shame even worse. Her own inner desire to have children along with outside pressures drove her to God's altar and she became desperate. She saw God as her only answer and insisted on a miracle from Him. God answered her faith and she eventually conceived.

After she bore her son, she sang her song about God **"It is not by strength that one prevails."** **(1 Sam 2:9)** When she saw that there was no way possible in herself, she admitted to an empty womb before God and grieved her barren condition. God answered her humility and opened up a way for her.

Because her son Samuel was birthed supernaturally, this made Hannah a prototype of the virgin Mary. This documented miraculous birth paved the way for belief in the miracle birth of the Savior. Because Hannah believed that God was her only answer, He used her life to point to Him.

Jesus said **"I am the way and the truth and the life..."** **(John 14:6 NIV)** We need to see Jesus Christ as our sole resource. Our very life should hinge upon Him.

Our faith becomes diluted when we turn to other solutions. We just don't consider God as the one we need to turn to or perhaps we carry a "why bother?" defeated attitude. Other diversions from God include 1) pretending nothing is bothering us 2) go on a shopping spree 3) always turn to human relationships for help 4) make ourselves too busy to think about our problems 5) watch TV or immerse ourselves in hobbies or sports 6) buy lottery tickets

Hannah's example of pursuing God is not very popular with us because we do not want to feel that desperate. Admitting desperation strips us of self-sufficient pride. We do not like to think that we cannot do anything about the situation or that we cannot help ourselves. The pressure of desperation forces us to lift our eyes off of ourselves and onto God where they belong. Then we have a correct view. Here are some of the things we see when we do not see Christ as our only answer:

Lack of joy	
Doubt	We see no hope
Discouragement	
Worry	
Negative speaking	We see no answer
Angry feelings	
Resentment	
Procrastination	
Giving up	We see no use
No urgency	
Disrespect	
Distrust	We see no good
Condemnation	
Accusations	

Our answer for all these maladies is to lift up our eyes to Jesus and to wait to see Him as our way, our truth, and our very life. **"Lift up your eyes on high and behold who hath created these things..."** (Isaiah 40: 26-31 NIV)

When our faith rests on God's power and we believe in what God is willing to do, then we can more easily wait until He does it for us. But, like Hannah, we need to press in to God when the pressure is on.

TAKE THE LIMITS OFF OF GOD BY SEEING
CHRIST AS OUR ONLY ANSWER!

---

* Are you looking to other solutions besides God's answer for the things that you want?
* Do you see your own inability to change things?
* What area of your life will you relinquish control and choose to trust God in a greater way?
* How has God encouraged you and given you hope that He is helping you?

A SUITABLE BRIDE

READ GENESIS 24: 1-27

The selection of a suitable bride for Isaac, the covenant heir, was critical for the fulfillment of God's promise to raise up a nation of people for Himself. The chosen bride was destined to give birth to that nation. Abraham delegated the job of finding her to his chief servant, a proven steward over all his possessions.

Abraham's servant was worried, though. Would he find a woman who was willing to come with him? **"What if the woman is unwilling to come back with me to this land?" (vs 5)** Abraham assured him that God would go before him to secure a bride for the heir. All the servant had to do was identify her.

The servant loaded up 10 of his master's camels with wonderful gifts to show the master's good intentions. They set out from Canaan to Haran, Abraham's home town about 400 miles away. When loaded with cargo, camels only travel about 3 mph, covering about 25 miles per day. They can go for a week without water, but when they do finally drink, a thirsty camel can consume 50 gallons of water to replenish itself. This trip to Haran must have taken 2-3 weeks. Most likely, those camels were very thirsty from the trip. So the servant stopped at the town well and began to watch for the son's bride. To test her willingness, he prayed that he would ask for water for himself, but that she would also offer to water the camels. No one would normally volunteer for this job because of the enormous work involved. Only someone who was hearing from God would volunteer for such a huge task. This would be the sign of a suitable bride.

He approached one of the women and asked for water. She gladly gave him some and then said to him, **"I'll draw for your camels, too until they have finished drinking." (vs 19)** At last, the servant had his sign. He sat and watched as she drew water from the well over and over again to pour into the trough. If her water jar held 1 gallon of water, she would have to repeat this at least 500 times to fully satisfy all those thirsty camels.

The servant was thrilled to find a bride for the heir. Rebekah had passed her test and so he gave her costly betrothal gifts and went with her to meet the family. She then agreed to go back with Abraham's servant to meet her bridegroom. The bride was found suitable for the heir on three counts.

1) She was hearing from God for herself.
2) She was selfless, exhibiting a servant's heart and was willing to obey.
3) She was willing to face the unknown and therefore displayed her faith.

The servant in this story represents the Holy Spirit, who carries out the Father's orders to identify and work with a suitable Bride for the Son, Jesus Christ. The Spirit of God becomes very involved with us when we draw his attention by having these same three traits. God is able to speak in a personal, undeniable way to each one of His people. The testing ground is our willingness to act upon what we have heard. Because it is God speaking, the task He shows us will be far beyond our own natural abilities to perform. God is looking for a reckless abandon from us to do His will. His grace and power will override physical restraints. The suitable Bride eagerly does the will of God, trusting Him for resources beyond herself. This results in a very super-natural lifestyle for those who are willing to carry out the purposes of God. Our eagerness to serve is evidence of our love and commitment to the Bridegroom.

The second trait of a suitable bride is that she is a selfless servant of all. She imitates the humility of her betrothed, choosing to put off the natural human spirit of pride and self-seeking. **"Each of you should not look to your own interests, but also to the interests of others. Your attitude should be the same as that of Christ Jesus: Who, being in very nature God did not consider equality with God some-thing to be grasped, but made himself nothing, taking on the very nature of a servant, being made in human likeness. And being found in appearance as a man, he humbled him-self and became obedient to death—even death on a cross!"** (Philippians 2: 4 NIV) Christ lowered himself to take a posi-tion that was beneath Him. As a result, God exalted Him to the highest place. As Christ's suitable bride, we realize the importance of the humility to do the task that we are told to do no matter how hard, obscure or undesirable and let God recognize, promote and further us.

In this case, the bride's task was to water camels. This speaks of our willingness to minister to people. Working with people is physically, emotionally and spiritually drain-ing. Often we are frustrated because they are needy, demanding, harsh, disloyal and ungrateful. Yet, this is our testing ground. God is asking us to love, serve His dusty, smelly, thirsty "camels" because He loves them. One of the Church's functions is to be the "water carrier" to carry the "living water" message of Christ from the wellspring of truth to thirsty "camels" who desperately need a drink. **"The Spirit and the Bride say, 'Come!' And let him who hears say, 'Come!' Whoever is thirsty, let him come; and whoever wishes, let him take the free gift of the water of life." (Revelation 11: 17 NIV)**

Thirdly, the suitable bride trusts God for her future and, by faith, goes with the Spirit where He takes her. We don't know how or where God will use us. We must be open to the challenges that God has for us in our journey. Our participation in fulfilling the Great Commission will take us beyond where we are comfortable and at home. We must keep in step with the Spirit as He shows us the next step.

One more interesting point. Those camels were the very beasts that carried the bride's treasure. If she had refused to water them, she would not have received the costly gifts they bore for her. Christ's Bride will be greatly rewarded in Heaven for her selfless serving of others. That, too, is a matter of faith. But this also speaks of the gifts of the Spirit mentioned in scripture. Spiritual gifts are not something separate from the Giver. They are evidence of the activity of the Giver. They are from the Giver's hand given as betrothal ornaments for the suitable bride. Rejecting the gifts means rejecting the Giver. The gifts should be welcomed because they are "ornaments" that not only make us attractive to the Bridegroom, but also empower us as Christ's servant-bride to supernaturally do a task that is beyond our natural ability. The emphasis should not be on the gifts but on the desires of the Bridegroom. The Spirit continues in this age to look for a suitable Bride for the King of Glory!

TAKE THE LIMITS OFF OF GOD BY OFFERING YOURSELF AS A SUITABLE BRIDE!

* Do you hear from God clearly for yourself?
* Do you understand how Christ lowered Himself to serve and save mankind?
* Are you willing to honor Him by serving others as He makes known?
* Aren't you glad and excited that He has set His desires on you?

ASKING FOR HIS INFILLING

READ EPHESIANS 3: 14-21

Our mortal bodies were specially designed by God as vessels or containers to hold the indwelling presence of the Holy Spirit. This gift to man is an incredible mystery, yet we know it is true because the Bible describes it and we experience it.

This truth is pictured for us in the Old Testament during the dedication of the temple that King Solomon had built in Jerusalem. When all the artifacts of the Ark of the Covenant were in place, God blessed the finished work by the intense arrival of His presence. **"When the priests withdrew from the Holy Place, the cloud filled the temple of the Lord. And the priests could not perform their service because of the cloud, for the glory of the Lord filled the temple." (1 Kings 8:10-11 NIV)**

Under the new covenant, God made the transition from indwelling a building to indwelling our human hearts. As believers, our bodies are the temple of the Holy Spirit. **(1 Corinthians 6:19)** This same entrance of His presence was foretold by Jesus before He ascended into Heaven. **"Do not leave Jerusalem, but wait for the gift my Father promised, which you have heard me speak about. For John baptized with water, but in a few days you will be baptized with the**

Holy Spirit." (Acts 1: 4-5 NIV) The groundwork of teaching that Jesus had laid was to be preserved by divine enablement. An astonishing flood of the presence of God invaded the room where believers were waiting as Jesus had told them. **"Suddenly a sound like the blowing of a violent wind came from heaven and filled the whole house where they were sitting...All of them were filled with the Holy Spirit and began to speak in other tongues as the Spirit enabled them."** (Acts 2:2-4 NIV)

This encounter with the Spirit was not a one-time event but instead served as a benchmark for all Christians to receive power from on high. The term "filled with the Spirit" is given to us with this comparison: **"Do not get drunk on wine which leads to debauchery. Instead, be filled with the Spirit."** (Ephesians 5:18 NIV) This describes a heady, uplifting, enjoyable sense of God's presence when the Holy Spirit comes to us to fill His human temple. From that infilling, we are then empowered to do the works of Jesus as God leads.

I believe there are three key elements to being filled with the Holy Spirit: Confession, Invitation, and Implementation.

Confession helps us to empty out of sin and worldly ways that form a barrier between us and God. We need to "clear the air" and be right before God on a daily basis. If God has convicted us of ways that displease Him, we must not fight Him or put off our repentance. Keep the communication open before the Lord through honest confession of what you know you have done wrong and what is bothering you.

Next, we need to welcome God's Spirit by inviting His power and presence to take hold of us. Asking for His infilling is much like driving into the gas station to fill up the gas tank of your car. Just as the car must be re-fueled often, so the anointing must come into us again and again as it dissipates.

Lastly, God's power will fall upon us only as we implement our faith in life situations. For example, when you go door-to-door witnessing for Christ and stand there grasping for something to say, the Holy Spirit will be stirred into action and will show up just as the first door opens! I find that every time I am scheduled to speak before a group, God will call me to prayer for a time of infilling. Then I can go out and do public ministry. When we put ourselves into situations where we need power, God is right there to supply it. He will override our natural inabilities and will supernaturally enable us to do ministry. Our part is to believe in His indwelling presence and then seek Him for a daily measure. He will see our need for spiritual power and provide the grace and gifting to do His good works.

TAKE THE LIMITS OFF OF GOD
BY ASKING FOR HIS INFILLING!

---

* Have you had an encounter with the Holy Spirit where you sensed His presence in your life?
* If not, spend some time in prayer confessing sin that may be known to you.
* Ask God to fill you with His presence. Wait until you sense that He has visited you.
* Get involved with Christian service, especially evangelism. God will enable you to serve with special gifts that are evidence of His Spirit at work in you.

CHRIST'S SIMPLICITY

READ PSALM 40: 1-8

During a half-hour bus ride home from work I over-
heard a man telling his woman friend about his upcoming day in court, the "pot" he used to smoke at parties,
his past bed partners, the child support he now has to pay
and all the other problems he was dealing with. I thought
to myself, "This is the muck and the mire of life that God
wants to keep people out of!"

The Bible asks a question. **"How can a man keep his
way pure?" (Psalm 119:9 NIV)** In other words, how can a
person keep himself unspoiled, uncorrupted, chaste, going
straight forward and stay out of trouble? The answer is
given to us in the next sentence, **"By living according to
your word."** By living by what the Bible tells us to do. This
way we can wisely avoid many of the pitfalls of society and
save ourselves much heartache from the complications of
sin.

In our meditation verse, the Psalmist confesses that God
lifted him out of the **"mud and the mire" (vs 2)** Like the
man on the bus, he suffered the consequences of disobedience that fill life with pain and turmoil. His life was a mess!
Christ clearly wants to simplify our life. He has power to
extricate us from further complications of sinful paths. The
Psalmist waited patiently for the Lord to do this for him.

Perhaps the Lord was waiting for the man to decide what he wanted for himself!

Unfortunately, in our fallen state, the human soul has an appetite for high emotion, forbidden ways and selfish passions. Too often we are thrill-seekers rather than God-seekers. Our unredeemed mind, will and emotions cause us unnecessary entanglement when left unchecked. Our passions may feel strong within us, but following them will only lead us to ruin.

We are told to **"throw off everything that hinders and the sin that so easily entangles" (Hebrews 12:1 NIV)** This verse implies that it is not very hard to get into trouble. Entangle means: to intertwine, to tie in knots, to involve, to perplex, to confuse, to trip up. Here are some common ways that entangle us:

1) The sensation of gossip
2) High emotion such as anger and hate, melodrama, and pretense
3) The pleasure of arguing and fighting to be "right"
4) Behavior to draw attention to ourselves
5) Vain imaginations about ourselves, conceit, fantasies about who we would rather be
6) Meddling in other people's business, trying to run their lives for them
7) People pleasing, living for other people's opinions of us
8) Living in the past, re-hashing what we cannot change
9) Self-pity emotions
10) Fretting over the concerns of this life
11) Discontentment, always wishing things were different
12) Power struggles for control, emotional "mind games"

13) Flirtation and teasing to arouse the interest of the opposite sex

All of these ways entangle us by confusing our mind and distorting our focus. Many of our relationships need to be looked at. Are we obeying emotional roles that we feel we have to play out? Are we bowing to human wills rather than God's will? Are we compromising our character just so that people will like us? Many people want to drag you down into the mud and the mire with them. Are you going to allow that? Other people purposely make us feel bad in order to control us with wrong intentions to use and abuse us. God does not want that to happen to you. What do you want?

Happy and relieved is the person who decides to do things God's way! We will find rest and peace when we let go of the sensual excitement that sinful living seems to bring. If we want simplicity in life, peace of mind and less complicated relationships, God will certainly grant us that! An aspect of the power of Christ is the beauty of Christ. There is an effortless beauty, rhythm and order in all nature. God is able to make things beautifully simple. He brings a measure of perfection into our lives when we adhere to His ways.

We need to withdraw from break-neck schedules and overly-involved relationships to learn to be content in the stillness of God's presence as much as possible. **"One thing I ask of the Lord, this is what I seek: that I may dwell in the house of the Lord all the days of my life and to gaze upon the beauty of the Lord and to seek him in his temple." (Psalm 27: 4 NIV)** Stillness within us and around us is a sign of God's abiding presence. This is truly the life-preserving stimulation that we want and need!

TAKE THE LIMITS OFF OF GOD THROUGH CHRIST'S SIMPLICITY!

---

* What are you doing or thinking that complicates your life?
* Trace back to when your problems began and seek God to make things simpler.
* Are you doing any of the things mentioned on the previous list?
* Ask God to show you His beauty, stillness and inspiration.

THROUGH RESPONSIBLE LEADERSHIP

READ 1 PETER 5:1-5

The key to successful leadership is wrapped up in Jesus command to Peter: **"Follow Me!"** (**John 21:19 NIV**) Peter's own failure combined with Christ's unmerited restoration and challenge to love and care for God's lambs intensely crippled Peter's ego. Peter eventually humbly emerged as the Church's foundational leader and here we read his instructions to the Church. This shows us that, in spite of our own natural fears and failures, God can use most anyone in leadership if that person resolves to stay close to Christ. Prospective leaders should keep one eye on the Master and one eye on the sheep at all times.

Why would Jesus make Peter so keenly aware of his undeserved position of authority? Because within our human nature, there is something about ruling over other people that activates the human ego. People in leadership who get carried away with self-importance can easily trample the sheep through their mis-use of power, causing widespread emotional harm. **"A ruler who lacks understanding is a cruel oppressor." (Proverbs 28: 16 NIV)**

Christian leaders should check their motives for wanting to lead others. Many selfish goals can arise that will spoil relationships. The temptation for personal power can be very strong, especially if there is a gnawing desire in a person to be great. Those who possess a dynamic extroverted personality may seek leadership because they enjoy having the attention of people and vie to be the center of attention in a crowd.

Christian leadership is also no place for us to work out insecurities and low-self esteem issues by trying to prove our own worth by manipulating self-promotion. Leaders should not strive to form a personal "fan club" in order to have followers dote on them. People who want to impress others with their self-importance have the wrong idea about their role in leadership. All of these motives are questionable because they are not geared to help the follower, but only boost the pride of the leader.

With these cautions, God encourages us to attempt leadership even if we are only a step ahead of those we lead. People are looking for someone to follow in life. Mentoring is an important means of fashioning the next generation for God. Christians should take advantage of the searching that people are doing, trying to find meaning in life. We can stand by with godly wisdom and advice, ushering them to the Savior. But our goal should purely be to build up, educate, encourage, correct and release people unto Christ. God will allow us to wield tremendous influence as long as we are careful to recognize Him as their source of strength and care.

Our passage says that we will receive a **"crown of glory" (vs 4)** for correctly handling leadership responsibilities. So what are the qualities of a godly leader? I believe there are four main elements that will make us effective.

The first is our interest. **"Be shepherds of God's flock that is under your care, serving as overseers—not because you must, but because you are willing..." (vs 2)** Are we willing to become interested in other people? If so, we have to be secure enough to get past what we are doing and find out about the gifts and strengths of others. We can encourage people just by being interested in what they think and who they are. Find out what is important to them and validate them through sincere listening and appreciation.

The second area is involvement which is mentioned by the phrase **"eager to serve."** **(vs 3)** This method of leadership can be pictured by a father playfully wrestling with his kids on the family room floor, bodies intertwined and weak with laughter. An article in the paper written for Father's Day by a mother who valued her husband's involvement with their two pre-teen daughters shared this observation: "A real father. The kind who was man enough to change diapers and endure the unexpected spit-ups. A dad who watched cartoons with them, and, yes rough-housed with them in the gentlest ways. Although they won't realize it until years from now, my daughters are experiencing a bond that will carry them throughout their journey into womanhood, and invariably increase their chances for a happy marriage."[7] This father's involvement formed bonds that will keep those daughters from disenchantment at home. In the same way, leaders who create interpersonal bonds, solid friendships and accountability ties help to keep people from straying away from God. Appropriate involvement in the Church includes phone calls to stay connected with people, sharing meals together, or going to seminars or special events together. Leaders can also offer their support when people are experiencing problems. Listening or offering to help through practical Christian service rather than preaching answers with reserved distance gives people the real help they need.

The third area is leading by example. **"not lording it over those entrusted to you, but being examples to the flock."**

---

7   *The Plain Dealer,* June 2, 2000

(vs 3) Leadership without real life experiences to share from is empty and unproven. When I first began teaching children's Sunday school, God gave me strict instructions never to require my students to do something that I was not doing myself. For example, I could not teach them the benefits of daily devotions if I was not having regular Bible reading time to tell about. Leading by example forces leaders to check themselves and not get carried away with setting unrealistic goals for followers.

The last area of leadership is commitment. This involves the personal training and discipleship of others in order to prepare them for their own area of Christian service. We should want to see others excel and actively work to raise up potential leaders. **"Clothe yourselves with humility toward one another."** **(vs 5)** When we are committed to seeing others grow and fulfill their destiny in Christ, the temptation to compete or become self-protective is countered. There is so much work to be done and genuine need for Christian workers, we should not waste time with territorial efforts to "guard our turf!" We should be glad that God shares His gifting with men and women and be committed to open every door of opportunity to those who begin to use those gifts in faith.

During His ministry on earth, Jesus reversed the normal standards of leadership which exalts itself above its followers by showing the disciples to exalt their followers above themselves. **"Now that I, your Lord and Teacher, have washed your feet, you also should wash one another's feet...Now that you know these things you will be blessed if you do them."** (John 13:12-17 NIV) True power and authority lifts other people up.

The blessing that comes from godly, responsible leadership is in the individual's potential to influence for Christ, bless, heal, and inspire many, many people. **"When one**

rules over men in righteousness, when he rules in the fear of God, he is like the light of morning at sunrise in a cloudless morning, like the brightness after rain that brings the grass from the earth." **(2 Samuel 23:3 NIV)** In this metaphor, the leader is like the rising sun signaling a new day (hope), who has the ability to shine over a given group of people, bringing light (wisdom and guidance), warmth (encouragement and approval), and growth (teaching and training). When people have a living example of Christ, they will mimic behavior they see and eventually become bold enough to try things for themselves.

Male authority figures especially have opportunities to bring healing due to abuse or absent authority in today's homes. The "father wounds" that people in our society suffer from is staggering. Yet I have witnessed public apologies made by courageous, sensitive, humble men who want to make things right. I have seen forgiveness and healing break out in audiences because men have been vulnerable enough to say "I'm sorry that you have been hurt" to a crowd of strangers. Male leaders can bring restoration when they position themselves as a type of father to those God gives them.

Mature, stable, godly leaders are able to build up many with the Christ-lead message they impart. God's refreshing will come through those who appropriately handle their positions of power as they receive their cues from Christ. Let us not live beneath our privileges.

TAKE THE LIMITS OFF OF GOD
THROUGH RESPONSIBLE LEADERSHIP!

---

*   What leadership position has God placed you in?

* Have you unselfishly served others?
* Are you committed to seeing your followers succeed?
* Ask God to show you ways in which you are competing with others?

PURSUING CHRIST

READ 1 KINGS 19: 19-21, 2 KINGS 2:1-14

Our saving experience with Jesus Christ is just the begin-
ning of a life long adventure with God. Once we recognize
the moves of God, we no longer explain them away as coin-
cidences because we see that God is truly at work around
us. His touch, personal and convincing, has now taken over
something within us. Like a strong addiction, we decide
that we must have a special dose of Him again and again
in order to live. We loved the measure of Him we experienced when we first met Him and we must have more—so
we begin to pursue Christ!

A.W. Tozer awakened his students to the pursuit of Christ
by writing this: "The moment the Spirit has quickened us
to life in regeneration our whole being senses its kinship to
God and leaps up in joyous recognition. That is the heavenly birth without which we cannot see the Kingdom of
God. It is, however, not an end but an inception, for now
begins the glorious pursuit, the heart's happy exploration
of the infinite riches of the Godhead."[8]

The free gift of eternal life involves going on a journey.
We are not sure of where we will be going—but we don't
especially care as long as our Beloved takes us with Him. The
young prophet Elisha agreed to go on such a journey. He
was struck by the presence of God represented by the cloak

8 *Pursuit Of God*, P. 14

of Elijah draped over him. From that moment on, nothing else in life mattered. Elisha was now a pursuer of God.

His captivation with God was immediately evidenced by relinquishing worldly loves. He said goodbye to his relatives and to his worldly vocation, gladly leaving them behind after he said "Hello!" to God. The pursuit of Christ involves the process of sorting out and deciding what we love the most. We inwardly choose our object of passion, shifting from the gain of this world to gaining Christ.

Worldly possessions have the luring ability to possess us. Anyone who participates in an expensive hobby can tell you about the investment of time and money to pursue that hobby. People pursue worldly loves because they become an extension of their own selves. When someone tosses his head back to tell you, "I love gardening!" or "I love golfing!" in effect they are saying, "This is who I am and what I have become!" That worldly love has become a summary of self expressing the identity of that person. We glory in what we see ourselves doing, so we glory in the object because it seems to represent us.

As Christians, we can't allow worldly loves to rule our existence because they don't last and they don't normally have a value for God's kingdom. In our decision process, at some point we must turn our head and pay attention to what we see God doing, and then leave our other loves to go follow Him. After awhile, those loves will fade in glory. We will look back and wonder what we ever saw in them because they don't compare with what we have gained in Christ.

Elisha showed wisdom by remaining rigidly undistracted in his pursuit of God. Even when his mentor chided him, **"Stay here; the Lord has sent me to Bethel." (2 Kings 2:2 NIV)** But the young prophet's pulse only quickened. He thought, "If the Lord is going to be in Bethel—then I'm going there to find Him." God saw the focused intentions of His young pursuer and He made a way for him. **"So they went to Bethel" (vs 2)**

Our spiritual maturity develops when we want God for Himself—no urgent need, no saving cause. We just like to be with Him. Having Him close is important to us. When we haven't heard from Him after a couple of days of Bible reading, then we begin to miss Him. "Where are you?" we question. "I haven't seen you in awhile. I want to hear from you again!" God is not coy or playing games, but lag time in His visits is our cue to pursue. So we press in harder to find Him as our prayer time extends and our personal worship heightens until He finally steps in to show Himself. There is nothing wrong with wanting to "feel" God. In fact, it is a healthy sign that our spirit desires close contact with the Holy Spirit. Wanting God's Spirit, which is the cloak of His presence, is in essence wanting God.

God will not frustrate His pursuers mainly because their heart motives are so legitimate. Enemy forces may try to deter pursuers because they cannot abide the fragrance of passionate love for God. Evil spiritual forces do whatever they can to suffocate and extinguish that flame. But if we avoid distractions and remain in hot pursuit on our journey, God will perform breakthroughs to make sure His pursuers get what they have traveled for. **"You have asked a difficult thing,' Elijah said, 'yet if you see me when I am taken from you, it will be yours—otherwise not.'" (vs 10)** The Spirit of God did not hold Himself back from Elisha's pursuit indefinitely. At last Elisha apprehended the coveted mantle—even a "double portion" for himself. This is explained by Jesus' teaching, **"Everyone who has will be given more, and he will have in abundance." (Matthew 25:29 NIV)**

To wear the mantle of the presence of God is the most prized possession that a mortal can ever have. God wants to drape us in His presence. Our singular love and active pursuit of Him is the pivotal factor for apprehending Him. After all, He promises, **"For the Lord searches every heart and understands every motive behind the thoughts. If you seek him, he will be found by you..."** (1 Chronicles 28:9 NIV)

TAKE THE LIMITS OFF OF GOD BY PURSUING CHRIST!

---

* Think about the time when you first met Christ. Have you strayed from your first love?
* What worldly loves compete with a sell-out commitment to Christ?
* Do you long for a greater sense of God's presence?
* How will you pursue Christ in a new way?

BROKENNESS

READ MATTHEW 21: 1-17

Jesus Christ is both the "Lion" and the "Lamb." Here is a back-to-back example of both the gentle, accepting, condescending nature of Christ (the Lamb of God) and the fearful, roaring, disruptive man-hunter! (the Lion of Judah) What, then, is the right approach that a child of God can make to One who has promised to once more shake the heavens and the earth, with plans to eventually reduce the stability of all created things to nothing? **"Therefore, since we are receiving a kingdom that cannot be shaken, let us be thankful, and so worship God acceptably with reverence and awe, for our God is a consuming fire." (Hebrews 12: 25-29 NIV)**

The approach that God has chosen for His people is brokenness. Brokenness is the total loss of dependency on self. In our passage, the blind and lame came to Jesus and He gladly healed them in their need. But the self-righteous priests were indignant when they saw the wonderful things that Jesus did and the praise He was receiving. By admitting out human needs, we learn to approach God not to impress Him but to implore Him!

Jesus never promised that our lives would go untouched by difficulties. **"In this world you will have trouble. But take heart! I have overcome the world." (John 16: 33 NIV)** The One who brings us perfect peace **(John 14:27 NIV)** will also bring us perfect disruptions! The troubles that come our way are meant to shake our own little world so that we will rely on Christ alone.

Christ insists that we gain experiential knowledge of Him. Feeding only the mind leads to selfish pride and arrogance. To know His sovereignty, He will purposely challenge our self-assurance and expose our weaknesses. The prideful trust we once held in ourselves is forsaken once it is proven to be insufficient. We will truly know Christ as Savior when we repeatedly experience Him as such.

Our brokenness is also meant to develop a personal sympathy in us for people who we identify going through the same problems. We can boost the faith of others by our explanation of how God brought us through. God longs to see the constant activity of people lending a hand, helping each other with God-given relief.

Personal brokenness is the forceful opening of self unto God. Normally, the self-centered life is closed and shielded by protective ways people use to resist conscience. When we are singularly focused on our own life, we are cautious to protect ourselves and become hemmed-in by our own self interest.

When we become "born-again," the Spirit of God comes in and infuses Himself with our human spirit. The two become one! This is a mystery beyond all mysteries, but is nonetheless true. The converted human spirit then becomes the means by which Jesus expresses Himself through the person's life. The hardened self-life that blocks this expression must be dealt with. Christ must often come with painful means to get the person's full attention and break the bondage of self so that He will be solely promoted through the individual. As the expression of self "shrinks" in abdication to the superior Spirit within, the Spirit of God has more room to flow from that believer.

As Jesus allows disruptions to come, several different awakenings can happen:

1) The emotions are played full range like a piano keyboard. We become keenly aware of ways that we are not Christlike when we see the ways we are responding.
2) Disruption is a test of who our faith is really in.
3) Our obedience is tested. During painful times we decide whether we will obey God or circumvent God's will to make things more comfortable for ourselves.
4) The spiritual lessons we learn during our breaking will equip us to be qualified ministers of the Gospel.

When we experience trials that reach into our private world, our response should be surrender to God's will. Though broken into pieces, we are softened as we yield. **"Everyone who falls on that stone will be broken to pieces, but he on whom it falls will be crushed." (Luke 20:18 NIV)** Rather than become angry and resentful, let those times draw you into loving God with a new zeal. Gradually, the penetrating efforts of the Lion will work the nature of the Lamb in us!

TAKE THE LIMITS OFF OF GOD THROUGH BROKENNESS!

---

* How have you experienced Jesus as the Lamb of God?
* How have you experienced Him as the Lion of Judah?
* How are you responding to God during trials?
* Will you let Him have His way through the breaking process?

PERSONAL SURRENDER

READ ROMANS 6:15-23

In his autobiography *Rhinestone Cowboy*, award winning songwriter, musician and country singer Glen Campbell tells of the reckless lifestyle he lived during the height of his music career, his addiction to drugs and alcohol, the people he met and hurt along the way, and the lessons he finally learned. He was born and raised in a loving Christian family and had accepted Christ at an early age. But his life bears out the truth that accepting Christ as Savior is one thing, while surrendering to Christ as Lord is quite another. If Jesus is truly God, then we need to let Him rule our lives.

To surrender means to release, to relinquish, to concede, to give up, to yield and to forsake. In the military it describes the losing side giving up when overpowered and conquered by its opposition. In a similar way, we possess a nature that is an enemy to God. As Jesus reveals Himself, we must surrender to the will of God, allowing Him to conquer self-nature. **"...So as to live for the rest of your earthly life no longer by human desires but by the will of God."** (**1 Peter 4: 3 NIV**) Often this is hard for us because there is so much fighting and arguing in us to have our own way.

Part of the ministry of the Holy Spirit is to change our desires. In our example, Glen Campbell used to live to sing, party, drink and chase women. As he has surrendered to the will of God, he no longer wanted to do those things.

In fact, he speaks boldly against his decadent lifestyle because his desires have changed so much.

Our verse speaks of us willingly becoming "slaves" to God. **(vs 22)** At first, this may sound awful to us. We think of a slave as a person who is wholly owned by another person and is under his absolute control. As Americans, we value our free choice, personal rights and freedom too much to volunteer for slavery!

But the verse goes on to say, **"the benefit you reap leads to holiness and the result is eternal life."** **(vs 22)** The reason why God is asking us to voluntarily become a slave is because He is protecting us from our own wrong choices. When left to follow our own desires, we would destroy ourselves! Think of the major decisions in life that carry the potential to devastate us by making the wrong choice: marriage partner, occupation, children, friendships, home, religion, education.

When we surrender to God's will, we are purposely limiting ourself because we trust that God's decisions are wiser and better than our own. Once we are convinced that God has a better way for us, we are challenged to surrender in moral issues also. We learn to stop fighting for what we want for ourselves and give in to what is truly right.

The decisions we make to trust God more and give Him more control in our lives release Him to perform in a greater way. When we surrender, we stop resisting the Holy Spirit as He approaches us to speak to us about God's will. We must let go of the selfish desire to govern our own life and enjoy the freedom that slavery to God brings!

God's choices for us are designed to preserve us, not destroy us. We will experience healing and happiness and be free in our hearts from the grip of sin.

As a fully surrendered slave to righteousness, Glen Campbell gives this final testimony, "I've been around the world as many times as most people have been out of state. I've been a lot of things to a lot of people, even when I was too little to myself. But I've never been happier than I am now." All told, his life as a "slave" is better, happier and fuller than his life as a "star."

TAKE THE LIMITS OFF OF GOD
THROUGH PERSONAL SURRENDER!

---

* Do you seek the counsel of God for His will before making major decisions?
* Are there areas of your life that you are refusing to trust God?
* How important is it to you to have your own way? Do you normally vie for what you want by fighting and arguing?
* Ask God to reveal ways in which you need to fully surrender to Him.

HEALING OUR WILL

READ ROMANS 7:14-25

Giving in to temptation was the downfall of Gennifer Flowers. She thought that telling her story to Penthouse magazine (along with photographs of herself) about her 12 year relationship with former U.S. President Bill Clinton would convince the public that it was really love.

In her autobiography *Passion and Betrayal,* she describes her mixed feelings about giving in to Bill Clinton's advances. "I saw him often after our first encounter, and he always singled me out and stared at me, as if he were trying to swallow me with his eyes...When he finally made his move, I had such ambivalent feelings. But still, I gave in and let him have my phone number. I struggled with the issues. I knew it wasn't right. He was married! But my resolve melted as soon as he called the next day...I let the urge to be with him get the better of me...Bill was really a master of his game."[9] She did not have the willpower to say "No" to what she knew was wrong.

Compare her inner struggle to our verse in Romans. One reason why we have trouble saying "No" to temptation is because the work of sin in us has broken down our human will. Compromise is the betrayal of your own self. It is having the desire to say "No" but saying "Yes" instead and then finding ourselves trapped as the door of temptation

9 *Passion and Betrayal,* P. 31

shuts behind us. If we are not inwardly supported by what or why we believe, then our will is undermined by believing nothing and we will cave in under pressure.

For example, I had a college roommate who was dating a man who decided they should marry. He was very strong willed. She wasn't sure if she loved him or if she wanted to marry him. But she married him anyway mainly because she was too weak-willed to say, "No, I want some time to think about my feelings!"

The work of sin makes us unsure about everything, like a compass spinning out of control. In Christ, the magnetic arrow of the compass finds its direction "north," giving us something dependable to follow. God wants people to walk out from under the power of sin by healing our will. For God to counter our slavery to sin is wonderfully freeing. We do not have to accept what the devil brings our way to trip us up. Through Christ we have the power to resist evil temptations.

We don't have to fall prey to the manipulation efforts of people either. So many times I have been angry with myself for letting people make me do things for them like the proverbial "doormat!" But God tells us that we should decide what we are going to do and then stick to it. **"Let your "Yes" be yes, and your "No," no..." (James 5:12 NIV)**

Often when we say "No" to people we risk conflict with them. People can put tremendous pressure on others to get their own way. We have to decide at what point will we draw the line to please people so as not to compromise our beliefs. **"If it is possible, as far as it depends on you, live at peace with everyone." (Romans 12:18 NIV)**

But if our "No" ignites a conflict, then the fiery furnace of confrontation will be used by God to forge our will to be even stronger. The strengthening of the human will this way can be compared to the process of welding two metals together. God's will is like a strong iron metal that cannot be bent. Our human will is a much softer, less pure metal. The welding process is done with a flaming torch, touching the softer metal and melting it to adhere to the new surface: the two metals become one. Our human will should become one and the same with God's will.

Our resolve to do right becomes a useful tool to God because it enforces the will of God on the earth. **"Our Father in heaven, hallowed by your name, your kingdom come, your will be done on earth as it is in heaven." (Matthew 6: 9-10 NIV)** People are swayed by strong opinions, especially if they are weak-willed and looking to attach themselves to someone with a stronger will. This is the key to Christian influence. People admire boldness, commitment, strong beliefs, and the will-power to live out those beliefs. God wants to heal the wills of His people so that they can have influence for Christ in their respective circles. We will be amazed at how strong we can become once we adhere to God's will and stand firm in it. This is the term "steadfast." It feels good to have the power to not give in to temptation and to live without the regrets that compromise brings.

TAKE THE LIMITS OFF OF GOD BY ALLOWING HIM TO HEAL OUR WILL!

---

* What are your greatest temptations that you are faced with?
* As God reveals His will, how important is it for you to carry it out?
* Do you give in to people easily when they put pressure on you?
* How well do you withstand the fiery furnace of confrontation?

SPIRITUAL SENSITIVITY

READ 1 SAMUEL 25

Spiritually sensitive people can "feel" what is going on around them much more than insensitive people. The invisible part of us, our spirit, has the incredible ability to sense and distinguish activity that is happening in the spirit realm. The closer a believer is with God, the keener that person will sense the direction of God and discover the schemes of the enemy. This type of knowledge is essential for breakthroughs in intercession as the Church advances in the spirit realm in spiritual warfare.

People were originally created to have an awareness of God's presence and communicate with Him in their spirit. The invasion of sin produced a barrier that shut of this tender communication with God. **(Genesis 3:9)** Left to follow his own depraved instincts, man began to resemble a brute beast in his spirit. **(Jude 10)**

The spiritual gap between man and God was bridged by Christ, who sends the Holy Spirit to a person who is "born-again" to re-establish that spiritual link. **"In the same way, count yourselves dead to sin but alive to God in Christ Jesus." (Romans 6:11 NIV)** How alive or actively aware we are of God often depends on our personal interest level. If we are more alive or interested in the things of this world, then we will be dull and uninterested in the things of God. The material realm and the spiritual realm offer opposite rewards and pleasures. **"No servant can serve two masters. Either he will hate the one and love the other, or he will be devoted to the one and despise the other. You cannot serve both God and Money."** (Luke 16: 13 NIV)

In our story, we see the sharp contrast in sensitivity levels between this husband and wife. He operates solely on the natural level while she offers herself to God's spiritual realm. From this example, we can spot at least four traits that will desensitize us to spiritual things.

The first is materialism, which is the modern term for the sin of greed. It is the preoccupation (if not obsession) with the accumulation of material things. As people scramble to fill their lives with stuff, God is shunned because His demands may threaten their lifestyle. Nabal had unusual wealth yet ungodly character. God strongly opposes this way of life because He takes no pleasure in being ignored, playing second fiddle to our love of created things. **"But God said to him, 'You fool! This very night your life will be demanded from you...This is how it will be for anyone who stores up things for himself but is not rich toward God.'"** (Luke 12: 20 NIV)

The second trait is carnality. Any person who lives by base instincts, momentary feelings or selfish cravings obeys his own flesh rather than God. **"In this very same way, these dreamers pollute their own bodies, reject authority and slander celestial beings."** (Jude 8 NIV) In our story, David made a reasonable request of Nabal to provide for his army of men. The appeal was made on the basis that David's military protection had insured Nabal's prosperity. But Nabal's answer to the request was, **"Who is this David?"** (vs 10) The issue was not that Nabal didn't know who David was. He didn't care who he was! David was nothing to him! Carnality is a lower nature that shows our stupidity, meanness, and lack of concern for others. Character is sacrificed for self-satisfaction, and it shows!

Thirdly, there is a lack of the fear of the Lord. Nabal made himself an enemy by insulting David and rejecting his negotiations. Nabal had no clue of the consequences of that error. Now David was on his way to kill him! The person who has no fear of the Lord has no respect for God's utter power and authority over life and death. **"The fool says in his heart there is no God."** (**Psalm 14:1 NIV**) Even if the fool admits to the existence of God, he denies God ability to deal with him. The fool thinks that there is no recourse by anyone higher than himself and doesn't have sense enough to fear for his own life.

The last trait that shows insensitivity is folly which is strange, silly, vain imaginations that put people out of touch with realty in their minds. **"A man's own folly ruins his life, yet his heart rages against the Lord."** (**Proverbs 19:3 NIV**) Foolishness is having childish, unrealistic demands and fantasies that causes us to misinterpret the way we see life. People can become so engrossed in a fantasy about themselves that they have no awareness of what is happening around them or how they are coming across to others. Nabal did not understand that he was indirectly being asked to help David's cause by feeding his men. Israel's future was as stake as Saul continued to rage against David. But Nabal saw no higher purpose in life than his own interests. He was stuck in foolish notions about his own importance and eventually lost his life because he frustrated God so much with his insensitivity to God's will.

As Christians, we do not want to frustrate and hinder the desires of the Spirit in our lives. In his book *Good Morning, Holy Spirit*, Benny Hinn talks about the importance of having a good relationship with the Holy Spirit. We are to know His presence, love Him, and "feel" or experience His activity daily. "As I began to know the Holy Spirit, I became sensitive to Him and learned what grieves Him—and what pleases Him. What He likes, what He doesn't like. What gets Him angry, and what makes Him happy."[10] He goes on to explain that, although the Spirit is the very Power of God sent to energize and bring to life the Father's commands, He is not merely an "unseen force" but rather an actual Person that we can relate to. "He can feel, perceive, and respond. He gets hurt. He has the ability to love and the ability to hate. He speaks and He has His own will."[11]

There are ways that we can develop our own spiritual sensitivity to avoid frustrating the approaches of the Holy Spirit:

1) Quiet yourself and spend time alone with God
2) Confess and repent of revealed sin to remove spiritual barriers
3) Watch and listen daily for the activity of the Holy Spirit
4) Appreciate God regularly through praise and thanksgiving
5) Develop an interest in spiritual disciplines. Choose to grow in Christ
6) Fear the Lord by admitting His power and authority over all life
7) Have a healthy respect for authority
8) Believe what the Bible says and let God have a conversation with your heart
9) Don't ignore God's directives. Make His will your priority
10) Get involved with personal and corporate prayer

---

10   *Good Morning Holy Spirit*, P. 50
11   *Ibid*, P. 51

Nabal's wife, Abigail, interceded and appealed to David on behalf of her insensitive husband. She knew exactly who David was and even prophesied victory over him! Abigail's godly sensitivity, courage and wisdom qualified her as a suitable bride for King David after Nabal died. In the same way, spiritually sensitive believers possess an exciting beauty for the King of Glory. God's people need to live on a spiritual plane first, complimenting the very essence of God. **"God is Spirit." (John 4:24 NIV)** We must learn His spiritual language, His pleasures, concerns and His ways. But most of all, we must recognize and steward His presence when He visits!

TAKE THE LIMITS OFF OF GOD
THROUGH SPIRITUAL SENSITIVITY!

---

* What has God's Spirit been showing you through your Bible reading?
* Are you obeying the prompting of the Holy Spirit or putting Him off?
* How has materialism crept into your life?
* How alive or interested are you in spiritual matters?

LIVING THE TRUTH

READ ACTS 4:32-37, 5:1-11

An alarming story from a national ministry newsletter reveals how common it is for Christians to be living a lie. The introduction of the letter read: "Maybe you know someone who has lost it all...because of an addiction to alcohol, drugs, sex or pornography...Recently we received a note from a pastor who had previously headed up a large congregation. He seemed to be a warm and wonderful pastor, and was well loved and respected in his community. On the surface he had it all. But what happened? He has lost everything as a result of a sexual addiction. He is no longer in touch with his family, he has been stripped of his pastorate and his congregation, and his reputation has been permanently marred."[12]

I am not re-telling this incident to condemn this man. The newsletter goes on to describe his counseling and gradual recovery from his problem through its excellent ministry resources. But from the description of this man's life, this was not a sudden occurrence. At some point, he must have decided to live two lives separating what he professed and preached publicly from what he was actually doing privately, and rationalizing that this was okay.

When the life we live in secret before God contradicts the image we are projecting before man then we are actively

---

12   *Freedom In Christ,* June, 2000

living a lie. Fake Christianity may look like ministry, it may sound like ministry, but God can't use it because it is based on falsehood. **"If we claim to have fellowship with him yet walk in darkness, we lie and do not live by the truth."** **(1 John 1:6 NIV)**

According to our scripture passage, two believers purposely created a false illusion in the Church that highly offended the integrity of the Holy Spirit. Their deception posed a threat to the tender new work that God was doing and had to be countered immediately.

In this account of the early Church, the revival atmosphere that began at Pentecost was effectively permeating society. **"With great power the apostles continued to testify... and much grace was upon them."** **(vs 33)** The abundance of power, grace and love poured out by the Holy Spirit had produced a high level of unity and unselfish concern for others in the growing Christian community. God was reinforcing the work of Christ and made His pleasure obvious by confirming the apostles' testimony of the resurrection.

Joseph was moved by the Spirit to make a sacrificial gift of the profits from a land sale. He didn't have to do this, but he wanted to as an act of faith in God and love for the brethren. He must have received some sort of public recognition from the apostles because Ananias and Sapphira were aware of what he had done.

Ananias and Sapphira also sold some land for a profit. But they secretly conspired to hold back some of the profits, yet outwardly copied the act of faith that had gained Joseph public applause. They were not required to give either but they wanted to make themselves look good! In the same way, the man mentioned in the newsletter in a sense lost his life, the consequences of fake Christianity were severe for Ananias and Sapphira, even unto death.

God wants to build trust in order to establish unity among believers. The Holy Spirit is drawn to people who are living according to truth, displaying sincere love, obedience, generosity and childlike faith. The presence of God cannot manifest amid fake Christianity because deception is from the devil. **"Ananias, how is it that Satan has so filled your heart..."** **(vs 3)** Lying and deceit destroys the childlike openness that God wants to create and maintain.

God does not want a lying spirit released in the community of believers because of its potential for so much hurt and disillusionment. Pretense is a form of lying. When a person pretends to be someone that he or she is not then that person is mis-leading others by putting on a show to look good. Self-deception is when we prefer to believe the lie we are living. Dr. Larry Crabb sums up our inclination to carefully select our own truths. "In its fallen state the human consciousness is a marvelous instrument of self-deception. It is capable of selectively attending to only those motives that preserve our cherished image of ourselves as good and kind, and disowning or at least disguising the ugly, self-centered objectives to which we are really committed."[13]

For example, King David chose to ignore the adultery and murder he had committed, using his position of power to cover it up. No one was going to question the king. When the Holy Spirit gave the prophet the wisdom to expose the lie, the truth finally penetrated David's mind and heart. In Psalm 51, David pleads for mercy as the eyes of his heart look up and meet God's eyes bearing down upon him. David painfully discovered that God looks upon the heart and has the incredible ability to see a person's inner reasoning mechanisms. God wants us to see our own heart as He sees it and to stop trusting in our veils of self-deception.

---

13 *The Marriage Builders*, P. 52

Contrition is not just being broken up about our circumstances, crying "Oh God, I wish things were better for me!" No, the contrite heart values truth and is broken up over what they see in themselves. "Oh God, I wish things were better IN me!"

God's truth and holiness go hand-in-hand. Living daily in the truth produces personal holiness. That is the life in which God powerfully dwells. **"The Jerusalem will be called The City of Truth and the Mountain of the Lord Almighty will be called The Holy Mountain."** (Zechariah 8:3NIV) Jesus himself is full of grace and truth and so will provide the power and grace necessary to live out the truth if we choose to trust Him. We can count on God to back us up when we resolve to speak the truth in all situations. Then people will trust and respect us for our integrity when they see that we refuse to lead a double life by living a lie.

TAKE THE LIMITS OFF OF GOD BY LIVING IN THE TRUTH!

---

* Are you doing anything to compromise your Christian life that could be considered shady or deceitful?
* Are there secret sins in your life that you are finding difficult to get free of?
* Will you make an appeal to God to deliver you?
* Will you make a renewed commitment to truth and seek God for His grace to maintain that standard?

MINISTRY OF RECONCILIATION

READ MATTHEW 5:1-16

The Church of Jesus Christ has yet to gain the center stage attention of the world that it is meant to have. This level of Christian witness will require countless peacekeepers within the body devoted first to one another and then devoted to the message of reconciliation for the world. **"All this is from God, who reconciled us to himself through Christ and gave us the ministry of reconciliation: that God was reconciling the world to himself in Christ, not counting men's sins against them. And he has committed to us the message of reconciliation. We are therefore Christ's ambassadors as though God were making his appeal through us. (2 Corinthians 5:18-20 NIV)**

In his book *The Body*, Chuck Colson explains that the Church is still fragmented because it has an "identity crisis." We have not fully embraced the fact that Christianity is corporate, therefore "the Christian life must be rooted in community."[14]

"On one hand, there is the Church God has created and intends for ultimate consummation. The Bride of Christ, spotless, pure, and holy, bathed in radiant glory and waiting at the altar for the Bridegroom. Then there is the

14   *The Body,* P. 56

present reality. Little congregations and vast denominations...Street corner preachers, Salvation Army bell-ringers and television orators who promise miracles for dollars. And most of them spend much time either bickering or ignoring each other."[15]

Sobering insight, isn't it? If this is true, then we are badly missing the standard given to us by scripture. We have yet to let go of "doing our own thing" because we see the greater vision of doing "God's thing," and doing it together. So the challenge is immediate for peacekeepers to come forth with their best relational bandages.

In our reading, Jesus saw the crowds and then went up to the mountain and began teaching the disciples. I believe that Jesus saw the crowds and knew that He was there to make their reconciliation to God possible, but He would not be there to personally offer them that provision. That was the ministry he left behind.

So He began to impress upon the disciples a radical new way to live that would keep them focused on the mission, curb their selfish pride, and unite them enough to create a movement that could be blessed by God. The Sermon on the Mount is distinct in its emphasis on blessedness. God was determined to make it clear, "If you personally adopt these ways then I can bless you." If something in scripture sets us up for God's blessing, then we need to pay attention to it. Let's look at each promise closely:

"Blessed are the poor in spirit..." (vs 3) These are people who admit to their need of God and others. Self-sufficiency was Adam's way after he rebelled. God wants to undo self-sufficiency. These are people who do not say to the other body parts, **"I don't need you!" (2 Corinthians 12:21 NIV)** They are not bankrupt in spirit. They just have a small <u>spiritual measure</u>. But they see that it is only a small part

15   *Ibid*, P. 58

and that fullness is gained by sharing within the Christian community.

"Blessed are those who mourn..." **(vs 4)** These are people who grieve over their true spiritual condition before God. They see their own sin and the sins of the nation and seek God's mercy. They will be comforted because they will experience God's willing forgiveness and acceptance of them, and they will go free.

"Blessed are the meek..." **(vs 5)** The world's way is to gain something for ourselves using forceful self-ambition. The Church needs to quit using this way. We are not building empires for ourselves. We are helping to build God's kingdom on earth. The meek, therefore, will gain the territorial authority of God because they know how to rightly and respectfully steward God's power.

"Blessed are those who hunger and thirst for righteousness..." **(vs 6)** These are not self-satisfied "churchgoers" who want nothing nor expect nothing from God. These are God-seekers who have tasted of His presence and long for more. They will be satisfied.

"Blessed are the merciful..." **(vs 7)** These are people who have decided to unselfishly love others. They show their gratefulness to God by showing mercy and kindness to others. They are compelled by the love of Christ to sacrificially love. This is the essential ingredient for true Christian community.

"Blessed are the pure in heart..." **(vs 8)** This speaks of our true motives for doing Christian service. Those who truly seek God's activity will recognize Him when He comes. They can distinguish between the works of man and the work of God. They don't want what is of man. They want only what is of God. Their motives are also pure towards others. They are not people-users, but instead they are people builders.

"Blessed are the peacemakers..." (vs 9) These are people who insist that God's Spirit rule and reign. They do everything they can to promote God's peaceful ways. They are able to diffuse anger between people and head off conflict by seeking God's will always. They pursue reconciliation and healing rather than enjoy the excitement of a selfish argument.

"Blessed are those who are persecuted because of righteousness..." (vs 10) These people have taken the words of Christ to heart and applied them to their lives. Their changed lives bring such conviction that people around them either love them or hate them. Their very lives become a decision point and a dividing line between those who will or those who won't accept Jesus Christ.

A community of believers who are committed to practicing these truths with the common good in mind would be invaluable salt and light to a society. God's grace combined with Christian teamwork would prove to the world what really works in life.

Forgiveness is one of the most important tools for peacemakers. Interaction between people is where we need the most grace. Conflict occurs when people are offended and then decide to defend themselves. Peacekeepers refuse to employ retaliation methods. Instead, they choose to forgive and absorb the offense by giving up their right to revenge. God is greatly glorified when we truly forgive others in the radical way that Christ forgave us.

To be qualified ministers of reconciliation, we must seek to have peace with God, with ourselves, and with others. This type of ministry requires much prayer, wisdom, patience, humility, and self-control. It is God's will for His people not to huddle in their safe Christian community, but to go out in the strength of Christian support, as ambassadors of reconciliation. God is asking, "Whom shall

I send?" Will you commit yourself to an attitude of peace and answer Him, "Here am I. Send me!"

TAKE THE LIMITS OFF OF GOD THROUGH THE MINISTRY OF RECONCILIATION!

---

*   Have you participated in any city-wide activity that has moved you out of your comfortable congregational setting?
*   Are there any Christian denominations that you talk against, condemning their ways?
*   Are you willing to work towards Christ's peace in your home? Your congregations? Your community?
*   How have you been an ambassador of God's reconciliation to others?

RELATIONSHIP VERSUS RELIGION

READ LUKE 13: 22-29

The greatest opposition of the Gospel in our culture does not come from the New Age movement or the cults. The great opposition is now bearing fruit from an ideology that was planted during the "Age of Reasoning" (1600-1700's) that caused people to value the development of the mind over the improvement of the soul. "The Middle Ages and the Reformation were centuries of faith in the sense that reason served faith, the mind obeyed authority...God's Word came first, not man's thoughts. Man's basic concern in this life was his preparation of the next. The Age of Reasoning rejected that. In place of faith it set reason. Man's primary concern was not the next life, but happiness and fulfillment in this world; and the mind of man, rather than faith, was the best guide to happiness..."[16]

I believe this ideology has become very ingrained in our thinking and shows up in an unholy combination of beliefs: Atheism, Humanism, and Materialism. Atheism denies the existence of God, capturing man's belief system. Humanism denies our need of God and its doctrine of self-sufficiency captures man's will. Materialism denies the value of God and promotes substitute "gods" which capture man's love.

16   *Church History,* P. 312

With the mind, will and very heart of man held captive by vain reasoning that opposes the knowledge of God, no wonder America is very hard soil to till for the Gospel.

To fill the spiritual void created by these systems of beliefs, many people today are turning to a "higher power," a nameless, faceless god who lays no claim on their lives nor makes no attempt to govern them. This "god" makes people feel spiritual, yet does not offend them by holding them personally accountable for their daily behavior. According to our scripture verse, people following this form of godliness are going to be sadly turned away from Heaven's gates when they die. Their empty religion did not supply them with a relationship with God. Only those whom Jesus knew as His friends on earth will enter into Heaven.

Religion is man obeying rules about God. It is a flutter of man's activities based on the false hope of man trying to convince God to accept him by what he does. Man is impressed with his own works and therefore attempts to impress God. So we see performance, not faith, is the standard for religion.

In contrast, relationship by faith is obeying God as He rules. Proper emphasis is placed on God's sovereign power rather than man's imaginative mind. Man humbly accepts what God has done through Christ on his behalf. While religion keeps God at a distance, far removed and leaving us guessing, relationship is God "up close and personal." We can know for sure that we have eternal life with Him and that the daily supply of love we experience is God's assurance of that unseen fact.

Most importantly, relationship is an honest person-to-person exchange. God wants to be involved with every detail of our life. He loves human life and the creation that He made in which we exist. No concern is too small for His notice. No voice too faint for His ear.

Relationship is also about communication that involves talking and hearing, not just formal silence. To know God is to begin to understand what He is really like. As He shares Himself, He reveals who He is by the way He chooses to answer us. Each new reality of God that we encounter awakens our faith in Him more and more.

Sadly, I know many intelligent people who do not know Jesus as a close Companion and personal Friend. They do not have His comfort and care along with His special daily reminders that He is thinking of us. Our priority on human intelligence potentially spoils a beautiful friendship that is meant to last forever. Don't let that be true for you. The following is a poem that expresses God's desire to have a close, daily, personal relationship with you.

A FRIEND FOR LIFE

Come meet with Me every day
And I will show you how close I am.
Come sit at My feet
And I will amaze you with the wonder of truth.

Be still at My side
So that I can whisper to you
Needed words of comfort and advice.
Come walk with Me through the meadows
And I will refresh your senses
With a bouquet of field flowers and grasses combed by
a breeze.
For I am the Lord, your God,
Who is much, much more than colorful sunsets
And rolling thunder storms.
Let Me show you all I can do for you.
By now, others have failed you or you have failed yourself.

Give Me a chance.
Trust Me with your deepest thoughts,
For I already know them.
Come pour out your heart to Me,
I won't let you sink into despair,
I have the power to hold on.
And in your most wounded hour
I will not let you keep the deadening pain,
Only its faint memory.
The pain I reserve for Myself.
Now walk with courage before Me
And when it is time
I will lift you up off this dull, brown, fading earth
And set you free to explore My boundless heavens.
I can do all things. I hold all things. I know all things.
For I am the Lord, your God;
Your Creator, your Savior, your Defender,
Your Best Friend.

Perhaps we need to re-evaluate our commitment to the Person of Jesus rather than to a form of religion about Jesus. Let's step down from the intellectual platform a bit to refresh ourselves with a new walk with our Best Friend.

TAKE THE LIMITS OFF OF GOD THROUGH RELATIONSHIP VERSUS RELIGION!

If by reading this message you have realized that you do not know Jesus Christ in a personal way but you would like to, then please stop for a moment and turn to Him by faith, asking Him to come into your life to show you His reality.

Here is a suggested prayer if you are not sure what to say to Him:

"Dear Jesus, I believe that you are the Son of God. I believe that you died on the Cross for the sins of the world and that you were raised to life again. I confess my sin before you and ask you to forgive me. Please come into my life and take full control. By your power, show me how to lead a life that is pleasing to God. Amen."

If you have prayed this prayer for the first time, you have received a new understanding of Jesus as your Lord and Savior. Continue to follow Him and God will bless you as you go.

PREPARE YOUR HEART

READ REVELATION 22: 1-6

Anyone who has spent leisure time fishing, hiking or camping knows the relaxation that comes from the soothing sound of a rushing stream in the woods or the cadence of ocean waves beating upon the shore. There is something about being near flowing water that is very healing for us. **"He leads me beside quiet waters, he restores my soul." (Psalm 23:2 NIV)**

In our verse, John the Apostle was given a vision of what Heaven is like. One of the things he vividly describes is the river of the water of life that flows from the throne of God. The source of this river is God and it is available to mankind because of the Lamb, Jesus Christ.

The water of life heals the effects of the curse, which is the existing state of sin and judgment of the world and brings eternal life evidenced by the tree of life on each side of the river. The leaves of the tree are for the healing of the nations.

The Old Testament prophet Ezekiel had a similar vision of a river flowing from the temple and producing the same results of life and healing. **(Ezekiel 47: 6-12)** These two compatible visions confirm the existence of a flow of power from the throne of God that brings life and healing from Heaven to earth. God wants to reverse the curse by His power and to His glory.

So the key question is: How does man access this wonderful healing river for his use and benefit? How does the spiritual river find its way into the natural realm to do its wonderful work that we so desperately need? I believe John the Baptist was trying to tell us the way by preparing our hearts through repentance. **"In those days John the Baptist came preaching in the Desert of Judea and saying, 'Repent for the kingdom of heaven is near!'"** (Matthew 3:2 NIV) The entrance point for the kingdom of heaven is the human heart. Repentance of sin is the key to opening the way for the power of Heaven to enter the natural realm.

God has ordained human agency to carry out His purposes on earth. God's power is meant to flow through man for the healing of the nations. **"Whoever believes in me, as the scripture has said, streams of living water will flow from within him."** (John 7:38-39 NIV) There must be a preparation of the human heart to make a way for the glory of God to come forth through it. John the Baptist made reference to this preparation as described in the Old Testament: **"... make straight in the wilderness a highway for our God. Every valley shall be raised up, every mountain and hill made low; the rough ground shall become level, and the rugged places a plain. And the glory of the Lord will be revealed, and all mankind together will see it, for the mouth of the Lord has spoken."** (Isaiah 40: 3-5 NIV)

Through repentance, we must allow God's Spirit to straighten out the crooked, twisted and perverse ways in our heart and remove any hard, objecting ways that would hinder His flow through us. The human heart must be dealt with before this flow of power can be released. That preparation includes turning our hearts fully to God until we see Christ alone as our sole motivation. Our hearts must be softened, even broken to remove our cold selfishness. Our hearts need to be opened to the ways of God, trusting, obedient, willing and attentive to Christ. And the Spirit must also reason with our hearts to convince us of His will to guide our actions.

Christians need to do two things these days to prepare their hearts. They need to look up and to look in. In other words, see God for Himself and also seek Him for His opinion of our heart. In his book *Holiness, Truth and the Presence of God,* Francis Frangipane says that there are two things and two things alone that Christians must know: "the heart of God in Christ and our own heart in Christ's light."[17]

I truly believe that there is a glory that the Church is going to be given to carry that will fill the streets of every city in the world. God's will is to make Jesus Christ known by making Him evident. The world will have to admit to the reality of God through Christ whether they believe and receive Him or not. This glory will be carried by individuals who have had their hearts properly prepared. As this mighty river is released by God through His people, the message of eternal life and healing power will issue forth from those who believe. The glory of the Lord will be revealed by Christians and all mankind together will see it!

TAKE THE LIMITS OFF OF GOD BY
PREPARING YOUR HEART!

---

* Think about how people need God's restoring power.
* Do you consider yourself a vessel for God's healing?
* Are you willing to allow God to effectively prepare your own heart?
* Will you immerse yourself in a great vision of what God wants to do on earth?

---

17   *Holiness, Truth and the Presence of God,* P. 20

MAKING EXCELLENT CHOICES

READ DEUTERONOMY 30: 11-20

If there was a "golden boy" of the Old Testament who seemed to have lived an impeccable life before God, that person would have been the prophet Daniel. Unlike many of his Bible history comrades like Samson, Jonah, Saul or even David, Daniel did not make obvious weak-moment mistakes that cost him. From what we can tell based on the position of power that he eventually gained, Daniel was blessed by God due to a lifetime of making excellent choices.

From the start, Daniel had many golden opportunities to forget his faith and indulge himself with the opulence of palace life. **"The king assigned them a daily amount of food and wine from the king's table. They were trained for three years, and after that they were to enter the king's service ...but Daniel resolved not to defile himself with the royal food and wine..." (Daniel 1:5-8 NIV)**

Because he refused to compromise his beliefs, Daniel was watched and seized, and then thrown into the lion's den. But when Daniel emerged the next morning untouched, he gave the king this simple explanation: **"My God sent his angel, and he shut the mouths of the lions. They have**

**not hurt me, because I was found innocent in his sight."
(Daniel 6:22 NIV)**

There was something golden about Daniel's character that God honored to spare his life. The Bible refers to it as **"an excellent spirit." (Daniel 6:3 NRSV)** That spirit of excellence made the evil men around him furious. But Daniel didn't care because he was living to please God alone.

From Daniel's example, a lifetime of excellent choices adds up to blessing, honor and favor with God. Not that we aren't allowed to make any mistakes. But if our mind is made up to make excellent choices, then we will recognize the perfect way when it appears.

According to these study verses in Deuteronomy, God leaves much of our future in our own hands. He clearly shows that it is His will to bless and prosper, but that we determine our fare in life by the choices that we make. So we see that God's perfect will for us can be severely limited when we make poor, short-sighted disobedient choices that are against His intentions. He says that excellence is within our grasp, and that He has not made it too hard nor placed it beyond our reach. **(vs. 11)** God makes His will known through the written commands in the Bible. Even a child can understand spiritual truth by hearing or reading what Jesus said. Yet the truth is so sharp and profound that it challenges young and old, the weak and the powerful, the simple and the educated. To follow the truth is not easy, but it is not impossible either.

"No, the word is very near you..." (vs 14) This means that God's written Word has been made available to us and, by His Spirit, God makes Himself available to breathe new life into us. We have no excuse not to obey Him. Then He gives a seemingly obvious choice: either life and prosperity or death and destruction **(vs 15)** hinging on a simple command, **"to love the Lord your God, to walk in his ways, and to keep his commands..."** **(vs 16)** To choose the latter choice seems like sheer insanity, especially when we can enjoy the reward of excellent choices.

Yet so many people choose the lower, easier, more popular route of disobedience that ultimately leads to death and destruction. For example, twin babies were born to a Christian pastor and his wife—a boy and a girl. Both children became Christians, both were very gifted spiritually and both went on to Christian college.

The boy was self-centered and abusive to his sister at an early age. But he denied his behavior and sought refuge in his parents who favored him and made excuses for him. The girl, on the other hand, hated self-seeking and only wanted to please the Lord in everything she did.

The boy began to see the excellent spirit that was developing in his sister, and he became angry and jealous of her. He eventually rebelled against his parents, defiled himself with immorality.

The girl gained a quiet, compliant spirit as she gave herself to prayer. Her beauty attracted a faithful Christian man who loved her, and became her husband and father of two blessed children. The twin brother's marriage was on the rocks and his home life was a wreck. He lost his job due to horrible disobedient attitudes and his health failed. His sister's husband prospered financially, as God opened up a storehouse of blessing for them. All told, the brother had to pick up the pieces of his life and the sister was launched into ministry with her family.

So what happened in this true life story? Did God show favoritism? He says that He doesn't. **"For God does not show favoritism." (Romans 2:11 NIV)** But He also says that

He will bless obedient decisions that add up to a lifetime of excellence.

In his counseling research, Dr. Larry Crabb notes the constant decision process that goes on within people. How we respond in given situations will determine the next step we take. "People respond to a significant interpersonal event with both a decision and an emotion. The decision may be to minister in spite of an offense or to manipulate because of an offense and the hurt provoked; because the decision represents a free moral choice, we must bear the full responsibility for the alternative we select."[18]

Dr. Crabb's detective work concludes that we are responsible for the choices we make, good or bad. As you can see, taking the limits off of God is truly an "inside job." We have many important decisions that God is watching us make in our hearts. He sees what really matters to us, who we will serve and how we have decided to live. If we truly believe that all of our decisions will someday add up to a sum total, why not add up to excellence with the one life we have been given? Why not value life enough to do it right?

If God says He will endorse obedient choices, why not challenge ourselves to be faithful, to be pure, to be harmless, and grateful and giving? How about taking full advantage of our privilege in prayer and see where it takes us? Dare to access the power of the Cross and live in the beauty and simplicity of personal holiness. Have the faith to remain steadfast, to be truthful, to pursue Christ above all else, and to look forward to the Judgment Day when you will stand with Him as a suitable Bride. Prepare your heart, and live to bring healing and reconciliation to others. You only have the delusion of self to lose!

---

18 *The Marriage Builder,* P. 40

God wants to be represented by people like Daniel as fearless men and women of excellence who give honor to His name by making a difference for God in their world. So TAKE THE LIMITS OFF OF GOD by making excellent choices. God can surely bless consistent obedience as you display your love for Him. And if you haven't lived that way so far, then start fresh today. Choose to make an inner decision to follow JESUS for yourself every day!

REFERENCES

Anderson, Neil, *Freedom in Christ*, La Habra, CA, 2000

Arnold, Caroline, *Camel*, William Morrow Company, New York, NY, 1992

Brown, Michael, *From Holy Laughter to Holy Fire*, Destiny Image Publishers, Inc., Shippenburg, PA, 1997

Campbell, Glen, *Rhinestone Cowboy*, Villard Books, New York, NY, 1994

"The Cleveland Plain Dealer," Plain Dealer Publishing Co., Cleveland, OH

Colson, Charles, *The Body*, Word Publishing, Dallas, TX, 1992

Crabb, Dr. Larry, *The Marriage Builder*, Zondervan Publishing House, Grand Rapids, MI, 1982

Flowers, Gennifer, *Passion and Betrayal*, Emery Dalton Books, Del Mar, CA, 1995

Frangipane, Francis, *Holiness, Truth and the Presence of God*, Advancing Church Publications, Cedar Rapids, 1986

Licciardello, Carmen, *Raising The Standard*, Sparrow Press, Nashville, TN, 1994

McDowell, Josh, *"Personal Truth,"* Campus Crusade For Christ, Colorado Springs, CO, 1999

Pratney, Winkie A., *Revival*, Whitaker House, Springdale, IN, 1983

Shelley, Bruce L., *Church History In Plain Language*, Word Publishing, Dallas, TX 1982

Tozer, A.W., *The Pursuit of God*, Christian Publications, Inc., CampHill, PA, 1982

Made in the USA
Columbia, SC
09 February 2022

55783814R00100